PENGUIN ENGLISH POETS
GENERAL EDITOR: CHRISTOPHER RICKS

SELECTED POEMS OF ABRAHAM COWLEY, EDMUND WALLER AND JOHN OLDHAM

ABRAHAM COWLEY (1618–67) was born posthumously to a London stationer. A precocious child, he published poetry at the age of fifteen and wrote plays in English and Latin as an undergraduate at Trinity College, Cambridge. When the Civil War broke out he wrote in support of the Royalist cause, and in 1644 left England to live in Paris. He returned ten years later and was briefly imprisoned as a Royalist spy. After the Restoration in 1660 he was supplied with an income by the Earl of St Albans and the Duke of Buckingham, but he did not receive the royal reward for which he had been hoping, and, in 1666, left London to spend the rest of his life in retirement. He was buried in Westminster Abbey. His best-known work is probably the poem *Davideis*, an epic history of the biblical David. As well as writing verse (he is the originator of the English Pindaric ode) he wrote prose, essays and plays.

EDMUND WALLER (1606–87) was educated at Eton and King's College, Cambridge. Married in 1631 to a London heiress who died three years later, he supported the Royalists and was even involved in an unsuccessful attempt to seize London for Charles I, an act for which he was banished, though he returned to favour after the Restoration. Much of his verse is devoted to praise, the subjects ranging from 'Sacharissa' (Lady Dorothy Sidney, whom he courted unsuccessfully) to Oliver Cromwell and the restored Charles II; it has been greatly admired for its smoothness and harmony. Two of his best-known works are the romantic lyrics 'On a Girdle' and 'Go, Lovely Rose,' both from *Poems* (1645).

JOHN OLDHAM (1653–83) was born at Shipton-Moyne in Gloucestershire, the son of a non-conformist minister. Educated at St Edmund Hall, Oxford, he published some Pindaric odes, but was better known for his satirical works, particularly his *Satire against Virtue* (1679) and *Satire upon the Jesuits* (1681), and translations of Juvenal, Horace and Boileau. He died of smallpox at the age of thirty.

JULIA GRIFFIN is a lecturer in English at Tsuda College, Tokyo. She took her first degree in Classics at Newnham College, Cambridge, and recently spent four years as a Junior Research Fellow in English at St John's College, Oxford.

SELECTED POEMS
OF ABRAHAM COWLEY,
EDMUND WALLER
AND JOHN OLDHAM

Edited by JULIA GRIFFIN

PENGUIN BOOKS

PENGUIN BOOKS

Published by the Penguin Group
Penguin Books Ltd, 27 Wrights Lane, London w8 5TZ, England
Penguin Putnam Inc., 375 Hudson Street, New York 100104, USA
Penguin Books Australia Ltd, Ringwood, Victoria, Australia
Penguin Books Canada Ltd, 10 Alcorn Avenue, Toronto, Ontario, Canada M4V 3B2
Penguin Books (NZ) Ltd, 182–190 Wairau Road, Auckland 10, New Zealand

Penguin Books Ltd, Registered Offices: Harmondsworth, Middlesex, England

First published 1998
10 9 8 7 6 5 4 3 2 1

Set in 10/11.5 pt Postscript Monotype Ehrhardt
Typeset by Rowland Phototypesetting Ltd, Bury St Edmunds, Suffolk
Printed in England by Clays Ltd, St Ives plc

CONTENTS

JOHN OLDHAM

ACKNOWLEDGEMENTS

Grateful acknowledgement is made to the following for permission to use the base texts, published and unpublished, all of which have been modernized, for extracts and poems in this volume:

British Library, London, for '[Sors Virgiliana]', from the Lansdowne manuscript 231, fol. 151;

Delaware University Press for the extract from Cowley's *The Civil War*, from Thomas O. Calhoun, Laurence Heyworth, et al. (eds.), *The Collected Works of Abraham Cowley* (Newark, DE, and London, 1989), volume I;

Oxford University Press for the extract from Oldham's Satire IV, from Harold F. Brooks and Raman Selden (eds.), *The Poems of John Oldham* (Oxford, 1987);

University of Nottingham Library for '[Sir John and Lady Denham]', from manuscript Pw V 431.

INTRODUCTION

The life of Edmund Waller extended over most of the seventeenth
century. He was born in the year after the Gunpowder Plot – a
violent, unsuccessful move by Catholics to dispose of the Protestant
King James I; he died the year before the Glorious Revolution – an
unviolent, successful move by Protestants to dispose of the Catholic
King James II. In the middle of his life came the greatest upheaval
of the century: the Civil War, ending in the execution of Charles I,
and eleven years without a king. Waller died at eighty-one, an
exceptional age for the period. Elegies by contemporary poets display
some uncertainty whether Abraham Cowley, who died at forty-nine,
had 'flourished long' or 'quickly gone', but his life had a similar
shape: its central year was 1642, the first year of the war. Oldham,
born under Cromwell's Protectorate, belonged to a different generation. He mentions Waller and Cowley (Cowley especially) as established figures, and he reached the mid-point of his short life eight
years after the Restoration of the King, one year after Cowley's
death. All three lived in a society highly volatile in the intermingled
areas of politics and religion, and made their own compromises:
Cowley, born an Anglican, wrote violently against the Puritan
opponents of Charles I, but lovingly and respectfully for his friend
Richard Crashaw, who had died a Catholic convert; Waller, born
an Anglican, directed his sectarian anger against the Muslim Turks,
and ended as a defender of the Protestant Dissenters, perhaps a
crypto-Quaker; Oldham, whose father was a Puritan, made his name
by attacking the Jesuits in the first year of the Popish Plot, a
fraudulent scare designed to rekindle memories of Guy Fawkes, but
soon seems to have lost faith and interest in it.

   Oldham knew neither of the other two. Cowley and Waller must
have known each other, though probably not well: they had many
friends in common, including Thomas Hobbes and John Evelyn,
and on at least one occasion they published poems in the same
volume. Cowley mentions Waller once, as a rival love-poet; he had

no time to read Oldham's work. Waller had time enough to read them both, but he apparently mentions neither.[1]

Cowley's personal testimony – of which he left far more than the others – suggests a life mostly unsatisfied. Of the three, he suffered the most from political vicissitudes. He began brilliantly: he published his first volume at the age of fifteen, and it seems that there had been plans to bring it out two years earlier. At Cambridge, he published a second edition of his poems, contributed to poetic anthologies, and wrote a play performed before the young Prince of Wales. Then, in 1643, he left his fellowship at Trinity College, Cambridge, to join the King at Royalist Oxford, and the story changes. He began an epic on the Civil War, which was supposed to celebrate the defeat of the devilish Roundheads; he stopped abruptly after their victory at the Battle of Newbury transformed his efforts into 'laurels for the conquered'. He stayed loyal to the Cavalier side, attached himself to the Queen's shady favourite, Lord Jermyn, and followed them to the Continent, where he worked as a private secretary and cryptographer. When he returned to England, it was apparently on some sort of secret mission for Jermyn; he was promptly interned by Cromwell, now Lord Protector. During his months in prison, Cowley seems to have finished preparing his first authorized collection for twenty years, the 1656 *Poems*. Its Preface sounds weary with defeat: seven years after the execution of Charles I, he urged on his readers the need to stop protesting and learn the 'Art of Oblivion'. Two years later, however, the Protector was dead, and Cowley saw that he had made, in political terms, another miscalculation. His old comrades were now in a position to reactivate their memories, and this Preface, coupled with an ode in praise of the Republican hero Brutus, had lost him the favour of the King – a favour that neither a fervid ode on the Restoration nor a renewed attack on the devilishness of Cromwell could regain. His luck had turned. The play he had written for Charles, then Prince of Wales, twenty years earlier in Cambridge was revised, renamed, and performed again,[2] but this time it brought Cowley an accusation of satirizing the Cavaliers. Hoping for a well-paid, sinecure public post, the Mastership of the Savoy Hospital, he reminded the court of his long service 'during all the times of distress and banishment';[3] in vain. Charles II knew something of the 'Art of Oblivion', and the post went to the brother of a royal mistress-to-be. Shortly afterwards, Cowley left London for a retired life in the suburbs. He never moved back.

The volume Cowley published in 1663 offered a range of thoughts on his situation. It included a reprint of his Restoration ode, together with translations of classical poems on the virtues of a secluded life, and 'The Complaint' – a versified dialogue with his Muse on his bad luck, which attracted some mockery at the time. In this poem, the Muse reproaches him for taking up 'business' in place of verse, without even succeeding at it. The word she uses is 'apostasy' – a strong word, commonly used for political desertion. As far as we can tell from his letters, Cowley did not feel guilty about his political career – he refused to apologize for anything more than 'error', despite Jermyn's best efforts to squeeze out something more mollifying; but 'The Complaint' indicates a feeling that his poetic career had also failed, and this did produce a sort of guilt. In the unlucky 1656 Preface, he wrote defensively:

as the marriages of infants do but rarely prosper, so no man ought to wonder at the diminution or decay of my affection to Poesy, to which I had contracted myself so much under age . . .[4]

His life had not somehow fulfilled that early contract. He was deeply aware of his own poetic precocity, but to him it brought a sense of frustration, even of mutilation. The first poem in the 1656 volume is a glum elegy in Latin, apologizing to the University of Cambridge, his reproachful 'mother' and poetic nurse, for abandoning her when 'step-mother Fortune' (in the shape of the Puritans) drove him from the city. In the 1656 poem 'Destiny', on the other hand, the Muse herself is a kind of stepmother, who has kidnapped and then 'circumcized' him; and in his essay 'Of Myself', unpublished in his lifetime, he makes the remarkable claim that by reading Spenser's *The Faerie Queene* (then some thirty years old), he 'was . . . made a poet as irremediably as a child is made an eunuch'[5] – perhaps as startling an analogy as any poet has ever given for his vocation. Poetry is a 'mistress, which I have loved so long', but she has not brought happiness. The direction of this imagery is confirmed by Cowley's stark account of the writing of love-poetry:

sooner or later [poets] must all pass through that trial, like some Mahometan monks, that are bound by their order, once at least in their life, to make a pilgrimage to Mecca.[6]

That goes some way towards excusing Dr Johnson's remark that *The Mistress*, Cowley's own 'pilgrimage', 'might have been written for penance by a hermit, or for hire by a philosophical rhymer who had only heard of another sex'.[7] If, as Johnson and many later readers have felt, Cowley's love-poetry lacks conviction, that may in part be explained by the link in his mind between poetry and emotional dissatisfaction. He was a hard-working poet: he was the first to popularize the English 'Pindaric Ode' – a combination of a grand manner with an irregular verse-form;[8] he wrote four books of a biblical epic on David, with commentary of considerably greater length than the text, explaining points of philology, versification, history, politics and theology. He was admired for it all, retaining a high reputation for over a century after his death.[9] And yet by 1690 his poetry was already beginning to seem old-fashioned; by 1700 Dryden damned him as 'a great poet' but not a 'good writer'; and by 1740 Pope, though still complimentary, could claim that no one read him any more.[10] Dr Johnson's lengthy attack on his 'metaphysical' style consolidated the verdict.

A modern critic has described Cowley as a figure of 'oscillation'.[11] Sometimes he blamed politics, for distracting him from poetry; sometimes poetry, for blocking his public career. The double allegiance gives him a partial similarity with his near-contemporary and reputed admirer, John Milton. Milton also dreamt from an early age of being a poet; he too made the choice to make himself part of his country's crisis, and so interrupted that dream. Both poets wrote epics reflecting contemporary politics in a cosmic struggle. Cowley's attempts petered out – *The Civil War* when the heavenly Royalist cause was defeated by history; *Davideis*, the story of God's appointed king on the run, when the poet's own 'leisure' and 'appetite' failed him. What he would have made of Milton personally can only be imagined (Macaulay imagined a lively conversation between them 'touching the Great Civil War').[12] Of Milton's poetry, he could have known the shorter pieces published two years before his own *The Mistress*, but he died about a month before the first publication of

Paradise Lost. That is a fact easily forgotten when reading the last sentence of the 1656 Preface:

I shall be ambitious of no other fruit from this weak and imperfect attempt of mine [namely *Davideis*], but the opening of a way to the courage and industry of some other persons, who may be better able to perform it throughly and successfully.[13]

As self-appointed John the Baptist of epic, Cowley's timing was extraordinary.

The long poem he did manage to complete included some political images, but was rooted firmly in the other side of his life: the private, studious, horticultural side. *Libri Plantarum*, his six-book Latin work on plants, allowed him to express his sheer poetic and linguistic virtuosity (the plants are all given classical metres suitable for their personalities), and also the quiet, personal charm that informs his private letters. Pope, after claiming that his epics and odes were forgotten, praised 'the language of his heart': a vague phrase, but appropriate for Cowley's later writing. For the ancient world and its languages gave him a happy confidence: he never sounds so relaxed or so intimate as when adapting Anacreon and Horace. The *Essays*, his most self-revealing work, are buttressed with translations and imitations, all praising the retired life, and giving it a dignity that might compensate for the various failures that haunted him. In the first poem of his 1656 volume, he proclaimed his ambition to be a poetic conqueror, 'The Muse's Hannibal'; in his essay 'Of Solitude', he praised Hannibal's enemy, the Roman general Scipio, who retired into private life after defeating him: 'and happy had it been for Hannibal, if adversity could have taught him as much wisdom as was learnt by Scipio from the highest prosperities'.[14] The *Essays* do not pretend that his own retired life was perfectly happy; but he managed there to make what peace he could with his Muse.

Cowley, Waller and Oldham. The order is in one sense perverse, as Waller was older than Cowley by more than ten years. By the time of Waller's death, however, younger contemporary critics regarded him as belonging to a later poetic generation than Cowley – their own generation. 'Unless he had written, none of us could write,' wrote Dryden in 1664; and thirty years later, when Cowley seemed out of date, Dryden still praised Waller as the first of the moderns, before whom English poetry was in its 'nonage' or childhood. In Johnson's *Lives of the English Poets* (1779–81), and later studies, Cowley squeezes in as the last of the 'metaphysicals' – a style that was flourishing twenty years before he was born. This is largely on the strength of *The Mistress*, which, as we have seen, he himself presents as a sort of poetic exercise; but even when he is not writing in the manner of Donne, Cowley lacks the 'turns', the smooth verbal balance, that Waller taught Dryden and his successors. Cowley's poetic career, so he said, was thrust upon him unawares. Waller's, according to John Aubrey's biography, was highly deliberate:

When he was a brisk young spark and first studied poetry, 'Methought', said he, 'I never saw a good copy of English verses; they want smoothness; then I began to essay [attempt].'[15]

'Smoothness', 'softness', 'sweetness': these are the words applied into the next century to Waller. He was not, like Cowley, a learned poet; contemporaries found him delightfully simple. 'He has a just claim to popularity,' said Dr Johnson, 'because he writes to common degrees of knowledge.'[16]

A modern critic makes the larger claim that 'Everything in his verse is accommodated to man.'[17] This refers to his tendency to attribute human qualities to non-human beings (for example, the 'amorous shade' in 'On St James's Park'), but it suggests something further about Waller – an easy adaptability, which carried him comfortably through events traumatic for the less adroit, more sensitive Cowley. He was lucky, both by circumstance and by temperament. His career in politics could easily have cost him his life: he became involved in a plot to capture London for the King, which ended in the deaths of two of his confederates, but a combination of powerful eloquence and the funds for a very hefty fine preserved him. After a year in prison, he went off to a wealthy exile, from which he returned to a minor public post under Cromwell; after publishing two eulogies for the Protector, he greeted the restored Charles II with an enthusiastic ode, and sat as MP again in Charles's first Parliament. As his enemy, Lord Clarendon, said, 'his company was acceptable, where his spirit was odious' (and Clarendon himself had a bust of Waller in his gallery of poets).[18] Waller was a resilient man; his 'softness' was different from Cowley's vulnerability. Clarendon opposed his bid for the Provostship of Eton as well as Cowley's for the Savoy: Cowley described himself as 'melancholy' and left London; Waller remained, uncomplaining, and led the attack in Parliament when Clarendon fell from royal favour.

Clarendon was not alone in regarding Waller's career with contempt, but that is not the only possible response. A contemporary, Sir Ralph Verney, records him as urging Parliament 'first look to our safety, and then to our honour';[19] Verney's nineteenth-century editor was disgusted, but these things have looked rather different since 1918. Set beside Cowley's poetic attempts to present the parliamentary leaders as henchmen of Satan, Waller's moderate speeches in the House sound adult and sensible. In his ode for the Restoration, Cowley developed a long comparison between the King and Christ to justify the exile, while Waller, in his, was content to praise the valuable experience Charles had gained. Cowley's own career illustrates the folly, in any but idealistic terms, of identifying too thoroughly with the Stuart cause. According to a famous story, Charles II remarked (rightly enough) that Waller's Restoration ode was inferior to his panegyric for Cromwell; 'Sir,' replied Waller, 'we poets never succeed so well in writing truth as in fiction.'[20] The scene has at least a symbolic truth: the two cynics understood each other perfectly. Waller fitted in well with Restoration society. He rewrote the end of *The Maid's Tragedy*, that stern old Jacobean drama, in line with the new sexual morality, and he was popular among the smart young men although he did not drink. The abstinence seems characteristic: Waller was reluctant to expose himself, to take risks – a reluctance which may also help to explain why he refused to publish satire, in a great age of it. He kept to panegyric, ignoring the satiric responses he often evoked (his 'Instructions to a Painter' sparked off a whole genre of satire), and maintaining a calm shamelessness which allowed him to reuse for the King's niece lines he had written for Cromwell's daughter.[21] Waller wrote poems about the 'reform' of poetry, but did not explain what he thought its function was; he did not share Cowley's faith in poetic inspiration or immortality. Instead, he worried about the perishable quality of the English language, which might soon make his work unintelligible. But he had his own sort of consolation, even here. Poetry, he says, will not have been 'in vain', so long as somebody is pleased.[22]

In the last years of his life he wrote religious verse – a muted reflection, perhaps, of the last-minute conversions of some of his rakish acquaintances. It is strange to think that Thomas Ellwood, the Quaker to whom Milton showed the unpublished *Paradise Lost*, also read Waller's religious verse in manuscript; it would be interesting to know how he rated them both. Waller had an active sympathy with Quakers and other Protestant Dissenters, whom he defended in Parliament. But Bishop Burnet, who thought himself something of an authority on conversions and knew Waller in his last years, described him afterwards as 'a vain and empty, though a witty, man'.[23] It is tempting, though perhaps unfair, to regard those late panegyrics on the Almighty as one last example of Waller's opportunism; if so, it is redeemed, poetically at least, by 'Of the Last Verses in the Book': a final moment of brilliant success.

Waller's 'softness' made him liable to a charge of weakness ('Ned Softly' was to be Addison's name for a feeble young imitator of him).[24] Oldham's critics blamed him for the opposite fault. The roughness of his rhymes could be illustrated from almost every page of this selection (consider lines 5–11 of the first piece); even his admirer Dryden acknowledged that he was 'harsh' and 'rugged'. Dryden thought he might have outgrown it in time. Perhaps so; but in Oldham, the 'force' that Dryden so admired is hard to distinguish from its jagged outline. The energy of his best poems is angry. The Advertisements he prefixed to his publications present him as a young man disinclined to be accommodating; to him, born without Waller's social advantages, sycophancy was a constant danger, and freedom a fierce obsession. He too was affected by the Civil War: at the Restoration, his father lost his post as rector and had to find work as a schoolmaster – a cut in pay that hampered his son's ambitions. And Oldham Sr. was an obstacle himself (Waller and Cowley both lost their fathers before the age of ten); at his insistence, John left university early to live with him, 'very much against his inclination', according to his first biography.[25]

Two years later, he escaped from his father into the relative autonomy of a school in Croydon, where he worked as an 'usher', or under-master. While there, he wrote a pious elegy on a school benefactor related to the headmaster, and 'A Satire against Virtue', a long poetic rant in the person of that demon aristocrat, the Earl of Rochester – 'not to flatter vice but to traduce', he insisted later, but also perhaps to express a fantasy of total freedom. The result was extraordinary. The unpublished poem reached the Earl, who paid the school a surprise visit, along with a party of dissolute fellow-peers, and gave Oldham the double delight (presumably) of honouring him and humiliating his headmaster.[26] Oldham felt enough personal attachment afterwards to write an elegy for Rochester, though he also felt queasy about imitating his 'bawdry'; there is no sign, however, that the Earl offered any other kind of patronage. Instead the young poet met Sir Edward Thurland, and moved from usherdom to private tutorship.

The question of financial independence tormented him throughout his brief career. Waller never needed a patron: he could 'thank inheritance/ For what he else had never got by sense', in Oldham's brusque phrase. Cowley, once presented with his Chertsey property by the Duke of Buckingham, was free of the need for further patronage. In his 'A Satire Addressed to a Friend', Oldham reflects that it would be nice to have a 'small estate', but that fate has not allocated one to him; nevertheless, he will not 'turn slave to eat'. The Advertisement to the last volume he published explains that the poems are not arranged with any care; if he ever republishes them, the author

means to have ready a very sparkish dedication, if he can but get himself known to some great man, that will give a good parcel of guineas for being handsomely flattered . . . This at present is content to come abroad naked, undedicated, and unprefaced, without one kind word to shelter it from censure; and so let the critics take it amongst them.[27]

It was worth something to be able to write like that; but how much? Oldham had in fact written flattering poems, though he had not published them, from which he must at least have hoped for something.[28] He refused to follow his last pupil abroad, which looks like a gesture of independence; but at the end of his life he was living in the house of the Earl of Kingston, 'with whom . . . he lived in the greatest esteem', according to his 1722 biographer. But then that biographer also commends the benefit to 'persons of quality' of 'a learned and obsequious friend'.[29]

His characteristic air of defiance is one feature which allies Oldham with that rising literary community later made famous by Pope – 'Grub Street', the world of hack-writers, enmeshed in 'poverty and poetry'. If his 'An Allusion to Martial . . .' is really autobiographical, as critics assume, Oldham spent some time in Clerkenwell, a London address a little way north of the geographical Grub Street, and well within its intellectual province. Dr Johnson also lived there, in his ill-paid youth; perhaps that had something to do with his plan (unrealized, but recorded by Boswell) to edit Oldham. Unless the opportunistic *Satires upon the Jesuits* are to be classed as hack-writing, Oldham was not a hack; but he understood their difficulties.

Writing was the centre of his life. He left little in the way of autobiography – perhaps the most revealing piece is a Latin poem in his autograph manuscript, entitled 'Mihi turpe relinqui est' ('To me it is shameful to be left behind'), on the poet's desire for eternal glory.[30] The life he wanted to talk about was the poetic. The extraordinary description in 'A Letter from the Country to a Friend in Town' of the birth-pangs of the imagination draws on Cowley's excursus on music in *Davideis*, and extends out towards Pope's picture of the chaos in which his hacks' writings 'like spawn, scarce quick in embryo lie'.[31] But unlike Pope, Oldham does not try to distance his own experience from this chaos. His poverty and his poetry were his two best subjects, and he wrote of both from his heart.

For their contemporaries, the image left by each of these three poets was distinctive. In the various poetic elegies published after his death, Cowley is praised above all for his precocity: two elegists go so far as to describe him as a baby Hercules, who could strangle snakes in his cradle. Waller was rather a late developer – a schoolfellow told John Aubrey that 'he little thought then he would have been so rare a poet'; elegies for him wonder instead at his continued productivity and undiminished 'sweetness' into extreme old age. In the best-known elegy written for any of the three, John Dryden praised the early forcefulness of Oldham, his unripe but 'generous fruits'; he was compared by two elegists (one of them Dryden) to Marcellus, the promising young Roman general lamented by Virgil.[32] And yet, for the modern reader, all three are probably best known as background pieces in a big poetic jigsaw. This Introduction reveals how easy it is to fit them in: Cowley, the follower of Donne, the forerunner of Milton; Waller, the father of the 'smooth style'; Oldham, the minor contemporary of Dryden, and perhaps an ancestor of *The Dunciad*. But their work has its own unique quality and distinction, which is beginning to be remembered. A fine scholarly edition of Oldham appeared in 1987, and a sumptuous one of Cowley is in progress. Only Waller, whose faith in poetic immortality was never great, has not been edited or published entire since 1901.[33] It may be that 'sweetness' has become a rather suspect poetic quality; but it is time that his 'proportioned wonders' were given due respect.[34] Few poets have summed up their own excellence so well.

Notes

1. Edward Thompson, in his edition of *The Compositions in Prose and Verse of Mr John Oldham* (London, 1770), includes a rather weak elegy entitled 'Waller to the Memory of Oldham, written at Wilton, in the year 1684'; but it seems most unlikely to be genuine.
2. Originally *The Guardian*, now *Cutter of Coleman Street*, performed in December 1661, published in 1663.
3. Quoted by Arthur H. Nethercot, *The Muse's Hannibal* (Oxford, 1931), p. 198.
4. *Poems* (1656), sig. a2r-v.
5. Thomas Sprat (ed.), *The Works of Mr Abraham Cowley* (1668), p. 144. The edition by A. R. Waller (Cambridge, 1901) misprints 'irremediably' as 'immediately'.
6. Preface to *Poems* (1656), sig. a4v.
7. 'Cowley' in G. Birkbeck Hill (ed.), *Lives of the English Poets* (Oxford, 1905), I, p. 42. Alexander Pope told his friend Joseph Spence that in later life Cowley 'showed a sort of aversion for women . . .' (Joseph Spence, ed. James M. Osborn, *Observations, Anecdotes, and Characters of Books and Men* (Oxford, 1966), I, p. 192).
8. 'The matter shall be grave, the numbers loose and free', as he said: 'Ode upon Liberty', line l.
9. See Jean Loiseau, *Abraham Cowley's Reputation in England* (Paris, 1931) and Arthur H. Nethercot, 'The Reputation of Abraham Cowley (1660–1800)', *PMLA* 38 (1923), 588–641.
10. Dryden does not name Cowley but is clearly thinking of him in the

Preface to the *Fables*: George Watson (ed.), *John Dryden: of Dramatic Poesy and Other Critical Essays* (London, 1962), II, p. 280. 'Who now reads Cowley?' Pope demanded rhetorically in his 'First Epistle of the Second Book of Horace, Imitated', adding that Cowley's 'moral' was still admired. In a later poem, he listed Cowley's 'moral lay' among the poetry that would survive. But survival is not the same as being enjoyed; and the 'main end of Poesy', as Cowley had seen it, is 'to communicate delight to others' (Preface to *Poems* (1656), sig. a2v).

11. David Trotter, *The Poetry of Abraham Cowley* (London, 1979), p. 134.

12. 'A Conversation between Mr Abraham Cowley and Mr John Milton, touching the Great Civil War' in *Miscellaneous Essays*, I (London, 1860). The form of the essay appears to be taken from Dryden's *Essay of Dramatic Poesy*.

13. *Poems* (1656), sig. b3v.

14. Thomas Sprat (ed.), *The Works of Mr Abraham Cowley* (1668), p. 91.

15. Andrew Clark (ed.), *Aubrey's 'Brief Lives'* (Oxford, 1898), II, p. 275.

16. 'Waller' in *Lives of the English Poets*, ed. cit., I, p. 284.

17. Alexander W. Allison, *Toward an Augustan Poetic: Edmund Waller's 'Reform' of English Poetry* (Lexington, KY, 1962), p. 31.

18. G. Huehns (ed.), *Selections from the History of the Rebellion and The Life by Himself* (Oxford, 1978), p. 49. He also had a bust of Cowley – described by Evelyn in a letter to Pepys, 12 August 1689 (William Bray (ed.), *The Diary and Correspondence of John Evelyn* (London, 1906)).

19. John Bruce (ed.), *The Verney Papers* (London, 1845), p. 181.

20. Quoted by Elijah Fenton, 'Observations on some of Mr Waller's Poems', in his edition of *The Works of Edmund Waller Esq. in Verse and Prose* (1729), p. lxvii.

21. 'Of the Lady Mary' (for the King's niece); 'On the marriage of Mistress Frances Cromwell' (for Cromwell's daughter: this poem is published by Beverly Chew, *Essays and Verses about Books* (New York, 1926)).

22. See the end of 'Of English Verse'.

23. Oswald Airy (ed.), *Burnet's History of my Own Time* (Oxford, 1900), II, p. 91. Burnet had orchestrated the deathbed repentance of the Earl of Rochester in 1680. Three years earlier, he had hopes of the Duke of Buckingham; according to a letter from Waller's dissolute friend Saint-Evremond, the poet was cynical about this.

24. Donald F. Bond (ed.), *The Tatler* (Oxford, 1987), II, pp. 406–10.

25. Anonymous, 'Some Memoirs of the Life and Writings of Mr John Oldham', prefixed to the 1722 edition of *The Works of Mr John Oldham, Together with his Remains*, p. iv.

26. This unattractive story is told with gusto by the 1722 memoir, pp. v–vi.

27. Advertisement to *Poems and Translations* (1683).

28. The most certain of these is his elegy for the child Katharine Kingscote, daughter of a local landowner at Shipton Moyne. Harold F. Brooks and Raman Selden (eds.), *The Poems of John Oldham* (Oxford, 1987), suggest that 'Madam L. E.' may have been Lady Estcourt, another wealthy neighbour of the Oldhams (p. 509).

29. *The Works of Mr John Oldham, Together with his Remains (1722)*, pp. xiv, x.

30. Bodleian Library, Rawlinson Poetical MS 123, fol. 104. This has not been published.

31. The passage from *Davideis* is included in this volume. Pope's description is in *The Dunciad* (four-book version), I. 59. See the discussion by Paul Hammond in *John Oldham and the Renewal of Classical Culture* (Cambridge, 1981), pp. 211–12.

32. See the elegies for Cowley published in Thomas Sprat (ed.), *The Works of Mr Abraham Cowley* (1668); *Poems to the Memory of that Incomparable Poet Edmund Waller Esq., by Several Hands* (1688); and the elegies published in *Remains of Mr John Oldham in Verse and Prose* (1684).

33. See Further Reading.

34. See 'Upon the Earl of Roscommon's Translation . . .'.

TABLE OF DATES

1605 Catholic attempt to blow up Parliament (Gunpowder Plot).

1606 March: Waller born in Coleshill, a village now in Buckingham-shire, to Robert, a landed gentleman, and his wife, Anne.

(?)1612–16 Waller educated 'under several ill, dull, and ignorant schoolmasters', then by Mr Dobson at Wickham; a contemporary 'little thought then he would have been so rare a poet' (Aubrey).

1616 August: Robert Waller (father) dies. Mother takes charge of Waller's education: she sends him to Eton.

George Villiers, Duke of Buckingham, advanced as royal favourite.

Shakespeare dies.

1618 August: Thomas Cowley (father), a stationer, dies. Cowley born in London to Thomasine some time later this year.

Beginning of Thirty Years War in Germany.

1620 Waller admitted Fellow-Commoner of King's College, Cambridge; no record that he took a degree.

1623 Prince Charles travels in disguise to Madrid with the Duke of Buckingham to court the Infanta. Their return without her is greeted with popular enthusiasm; Waller writes a courtly poem on the Prince's escape from a storm at sea (published 1645).

1624 Waller elected MP for Ilchester.

1625 Waller MP for Chipping Wycombe.

James I dies. Charles I succeeds; marries Henrietta Maria, daughter of Henry IV of France.

1628 Cowley goes to Westminster School probably in this year.

Waller MP for Amersham; sits on many committees, including one concerned with the 'Summer Islands' (Bermuda).

Buckingham assassinated; Waller writes a poem on the King's loss (published 1645).

William Laud becomes Bishop of London.

1629 Waller moves to Beaconsfield.
       Commons' resolutions against 'popery' and Arminianism
       (anti-Calvinist Protestantism); the Arminian Laud imposes
       censorship of the press. Parliament dissolved for eleven years.
1630 Charles II born.
       Some time in the 1630s, Waller becomes acquainted with
       Lucius Cary, second Viscount Falkland, and his circle of
       intellectual friends at Great Tew.
1631 Waller elopes with Anne Bankes, an heiress, and marries her
       against her guardians' will.
1633 *Poetical Blossoms* (Cowley) published.
       Waller's eldest son, Benjamin, born – he is mentally sub-
       normal.
       Sir Thomas Wentworth (later Earl of Strafford) begins admin-
       istration in Ireland. Laud becomes Archbishop of Canterbury.
1634 Anne Waller (wife) dies.
(?)1635 Towards the end of the year, Waller begins his courtship
       of Lady Dorothy Sidney ('Sacharissa'), daughter of the Earl
       of Leicester.
1636 Cowley goes to Trinity College, Cambridge. Meets Richard
       Crashaw (b. ?1613); they write verses for and with each other.
       Second edition of *Poetical Blossoms*, with *Sylva*, published.
1638 *Love's Riddle* and *Naufragium Ioculare* (Cowley: plays, one in
       English, one in Latin) published.
       Resentment at royal exactions (especially ship-money) and
       the policy of Laud. Scottish Covenant against the new Prayer
       Book imposed on Scotland.
1639 Sacharissa marries Lord Spencer of Wormleighton (later Earl
       of Sunderland).
       War with Scotland (First Bishops' War). Wentworth becomes
       adviser to the King.
1640 Waller MP for Amersham (Puritan) in the 'Short Parliament':
       makes a speech against voting supplies for the King. MP for
       St Ives (Royalist) in the 'Long Parliament'.
       Second Bishops' War. Wentworth (now Earl of Strafford)
       and Laud impeached by the Long Parliament.
1641 February: Waller makes a speech against abolishing episco-
       pacy. Apparently opposes the attainder on Strafford (not listed
       among the opponents, but after the Restoration he claimed

that he had to pass himself off as a known parliamentary champion to avoid violence from the crowd).

May: Strafford executed.

November: Irish rebellion begins. King's fruitless journey to Scotland celebrated in a volume of verse, *Irenodia Cantabrigiensis*, to which Cowley contributes. Waller obliged to apologize to the House of Commons for likening the behaviour of the parliamentary leader John Pym to that of Strafford.

Van Dyck dies; Cowley writes an elegy (published 1656).

1642   March: Cowley's play *The Guardian* performed before Prince Charles at Cambridge.

August: King sets up standard at Nottingham: beginning of the First Civil War. In Parliament, Waller 'spoke, upon all occasions, with great sharpness and freedom; which (now there were so few there that used it, and there was no danger of being over-voted) was not restrained . . . he was looked upon as the boldest champion the Crown had in both Houses' (Clarendon).

A Satire against Separatists (Cowley) published; Prologue and Epilogue to *The Guardian* (both attacking Puritans) published under a pseudonym.

King moves headquarters to Oxford.

1643   Spring: Soon after being made a Fellow of Trinity, Cowley leaves Cambridge, now under Puritan control; moves to St John's College, Oxford, where he meets among others Dr William Harvey and Henry, Baron Jermyn; becomes acquainted with Falkland near by at Great Tew. Publishes *The Puritan and the Papist*, a verse-satire. Begins epic on the Civil War.

February: Waller meets the King at Oxford, on a mission for peace. Becomes involved in a plot to win over the City of London for the Crown, drawing in his brother-in-law, Nathaniel Tomkins, and Richard Chaloner, a linen-draper. It is not clear how far 'Waller's Plot' intended to make use of weapons.

June: Pym presents to the House of Commons a report of the discovered plot. After a delay of a week, Waller, to save himself, incriminates other conspirators.

July: Waller makes a speech of apology at the Bar of the House; as a result of his moving performance, he is not executed but fined £10,000 and imprisoned in the Tower. Tomkins and Chaloner are hanged.

September: Battle of Newbury (parliamentary victory): Falkland killed. Cowley breaks off his epic.

1644 April: Cowley formally dispossessed of his Cambridge fellowship.

November: Waller released from the Tower and banished from the country. Marries Mary Bracey (spelling disputed) probably before he leaves.

Perhaps in this year Cowley leaves England for Paris in the retinue of Jermyn, for whom he acts as confidential secretary.

1645 Cowley and Waller both in Paris; seem not to have known each other, but had friends in common, for example, Thomas Hobbes and William Davenant.

Poems, etc./Works (Waller) published in London: at least three editions, one (printed by 'I.N.' for Humphrey Mosley) much the best, but all apparently unauthorized.

Prayer Book abolished. Laud executed. New Model Army established. Parliamentary triumph at Naseby; end of the First Civil War.

1646 Waller travels in Italy and Switzerland with John Evelyn.

October: Waller returns to Paris, where he remains for five years, the wealthiest of the English exiles except for Jermyn. Cowley employed on official business in Paris and in Jersey. King takes refuge with Scots; Oxford surrenders.

1647 *The Mistress* (Cowley) published in London – unauthorized. King is given up to Parliament; is seized by the army; negotiates with both, and escapes to the Isle of Wight, where he makes a secret deal with the Scots.

Beaumont and Fletcher Folio *Comedies and Tragedies* published with commendatory verse by Waller.

1648 Second Civil War. Army seizes King again, and enters London. Thirty Years War ends with the Treaty of Westphalia.

1649 January: King tried and executed.

Charles II proclaimed King in Scotland; Rump Parliament proclaims Commonwealth in England, and sends Oliver Cromwell to reconquer Ireland.

Crashaw, now a Catholic convert, dies in Italy; Cowley writes an elegy for him (published 1656).

Queen Regent of France withdraws from Paris; city blockaded in first Fronde (civil disturbance).

1650 *The Guardian* published in London – unauthorized.

Charles II accepts Scottish Covenant. Cowley, in France, writes to Henry Bennet of the Scots: 'he that will undertake to comprehend these men's actions . . . the next task I would set him upon, should be to write a comment[ary] on the *Revelation*' (*Miscellanea Aulica*).

Cowley and Waller publish commendatory poems for William Davenant's unfinished epic poem *Gondibert* – it is treated very roughly by other poets.

Cromwell returns from Ireland; Parliament sends him to Scotland as Lord General.

1651 Charles II crowned at Scone. Defeated at the Battle of Worcester, he becomes a fugitive and Scotland is conquered. Second Fronde (the 'Princes' Fronde') begins in France.

November: In answer to his 'humble petition', Parliament resolves that Waller's sentence of exile should be revoked and a pardon granted.

1652 January: Waller leaves Paris and returns home to Beaconsfield. France officially recognizes the Commonwealth. End of war with Ireland. First Dutch War begins.

1653 April: Anne Waller (mother) dies.

August: Oldham born at Shipton Moyne, Gloucestershire, to John Oldham, later rector of Long Newnton, Wiltshire.

Dorothy Osborne reports that Waller is planning to write a 'romance' on the Civil War.

Cromwell expels Parliament and establishes himself as Lord Protector. Treaty of Westminster ends Dutch War. End of the Fronde.

1654 May: Cowley, apparently on a secret mission from Jermyn, is granted permission to return to England.

1655 April: Cowley arrested in London with other suspected Royalists. Examined by Cromwell at Whitehall; 'he saw it was impossible for him to pursue the ends for which he came hither, if he did not make some kind of declaration of his peaceable intentions' (Sprat). Released; subsequently regarded with suspicion by Charles II.

June: Letter from Cromwell to Waller thanking him for 'verses' – probably 'A Panegyric to my Lord Protector', published in this year.

December: Waller appointed a Commissioner for Trade.

Cromwell appoints eleven major-generals to rule England and Wales. War with Spain begins.

1656 *Poems* (Cowley) published in London, comprising *Miscellanies*, *The Mistress*, *Pindaric Odes* and *Davideis*. Preface declares: 'when the event of battle, and the unaccountable Will of God has determined the controversy, and that we have submitted to the conditions of the Conqueror, we must lay down our pens as well as arms . . . we are all bound to desire . . . the Art of Oblivion'.

End of major-generals' rule.

1657 Cowley incorporated at Oxford as Doctor of Physic. Friendship begins probably in this year with the second Duke of Buckingham and with Thomas Sprat, future historian of the Royal Society.

Cromwell declines Parliament's *Advice* to become King.

William Harvey dies.

1658 April: Probably in this month, Waller publishes poem *Of a War with Spain*, suggesting that Cromwell should become King.

September: Cromwell dies. Richard Cromwell becomes Protector.

1659 Waller publishes an elegy for Cromwell; according to Anthony à Wood, Cowley also wrote one (not extant, if so).

Cowley returns to France, to find himself out of favour with Charles II.

End of Protectorate. General Monk leads army down from Scotland.

1660 May: Charles II, proclaimed King, reaches London. Waller and Cowley publish panegyrics; Waller's appears one day before Cowley's.

November–December: Royal Society established: Cowley included in the original list of forty possible members; his *A Proposition for the Advancement of Learning*, composed a few years earlier, is discussed by the Society.

1661   Cowley and Waller elected to the Royal Society. Cowley never attends any meetings; Waller attends quite regularly for the first three years.

Cowley publishes *A Proposition* and also *A Discourse by Way of Vision* . . . – an attack on Oliver Cromwell. Reinstated in his fellowship at Trinity. Requests the Mastership of the Savoy (a lucrative sinecure); said to have been opposed by the Earl of Clarendon, the King's chief minister. *Cutter of Coleman Street*, a revised version of *The Guardian*, is performed by his friend Davenant's theatre company (December); mixed reaction apparently on first night, but runs for a whole week.

Waller MP for Hastings (Cinque Ports). Plays important role in parliamentary business; recognized as an authority on procedure. Publishes 'On St James's Park', in praise of alterations made there by royal command, together with his poem on the war with Spain, minus suggestion about Cromwell's kingship. 'Clarendon Code' imposes harsh penalties on Protestant Dissenters; Waller pleads in Parliament for toleration. Around this time he is said have been blocked by Clarendon in his request for the Provostship of Eton.

1662   *Libri Plantarum II* (Cowley) published.

Waller translates Act I of Corneille's *Pompée* in a composite translation involving Sir Charles Sedley and others (published 1664). Possibly rewrites Act V of Beaumont and Fletcher's *The Maid's Tragedy* (published 1690; masque for the new act published anonymously in ?1683).

The wit and essayist Saint-Evremond, obliged to leave France after a political indiscretion, settles in England; becomes a particular friend of Cowley and Waller.

Oldham's father dismissed from his rectory as part of new church settlement; becomes a headmaster.

King marries Catherine of Braganza. Prayer Book published.

1663   *Cutter of Colman Street* published, with an indignant preface vindicating it from being 'abuse and satire against the King's party'. The Savoy awarded to Dr Henry Killigrew, whose sister is later mistress to the King. *Verses Written upon Several Occasions* includes 'The Complaint', inspired by this loss. Cowley moves from London to Barn Elms, a suburb near Putney.

March: Waller and Sir John Denham asked to give their opinions on *The Cheats*, a politically sensitive play by John Wilson.

1664 *Poems, etc.* (Waller) published: the first authorized collection (most of the poems in it were first published in 1645).

December: Royal Society appoints a committee 'for improving the English language': Waller is elected, with Dryden, Evelyn and others (nothing seems to have come of this).

1665 *Upon Her Majesty's New Buildings at Somerset House* (Waller) published; according to the Stationers' Register, Cowley and Waller entered poems on this topic together, but no copy of Cowley's seems to have survived. Waller publishes *Instructions to a Painter* (first version), and, in Sir William Killigrew's volume *Three Plays*, a defence of Killigrew's tragedy *Pandora*.

Cowley moves to Chertsey, where he lives as a gentleman farmer, enriched by land grants from the Crown, his rent apparently paid by the Duke of Buckingham. Writes *Essays* and the last four books of the *Libri Plantarum* (all published 1668).

Great Plague breaks out. Second Dutch War begins.

1666 Waller, with Sir John Denham, a vigorous promoter of the impeachment of Clarendon.

The Great Fire destroys much of London.

1667 July: Cowley dies at Chertsey. Buried in Westminster Abbey; monument put up by Buckingham. Sprat's *History of the Royal Society* includes Cowley's ode on it.

Second Dutch War reaches inconclusive end. Clarendon goes into exile. First edition of Milton's *Paradise Lost* published (in ten books).

1668 Sprat publishes *The Works of Mr Abraham Cowley* and *Poemata Latina*, with introductory biographies of Cowley in English and Latin.

1670 June: Oldham matriculates at St Edmund Hall, Oxford.

July: Waller, apparently made drunk at a party of Lord St Albans (formerly Jermyn), has a fall; seems in general to have been popular among the young and fashionable despite being a 'water-drinker'.

Second Conventicle Act: persecution of Dissenters again acute.

1671   October: Waller writes to an unknown correspondent for information about material from the Long Parliament, 'especially in the years 43 and 44 in the knowledge whereof I am at present very much concerned'.

1673   February: Waller supports a bill for the relief of Dissenters; it is defeated.

March: Oldham writes memorial verses for John Friend.

October: Waller supports the Duke of York's proposed marriage to the Catholic Mary of Modena.

Test Act excludes Catholics from public office.

1674   Oldham returns from Oxford (without a BA) to Shipton Moyne, where he lives with his father 'much against his inclination' (1722 memoir).

Statue of Charles I erected at Charing Cross; Waller writes a poem in celebration (published 1690).

Beginnings of a two-party system in Parliament: Tories, led by the Earl of Danby; Whigs, led by the Earl of Shaftesbury.

Paradise Lost (twelve-book version) published.

1676   Oldham becomes an usher at Whitgift School, Croydon. Sought out by the Earl of Rochester, who has seen his 'A Satire against Virtue' in manuscript.

1677   Mary Waller (wife) dies. Waller retires to Hall Barn. First surviving letters from Waller to the court beauty Mrs Middleton, also a friend of Saint-Evremond.

Upon the Marriage of the Prince of Orange with the Lady Mary (Oldham) and *Of the Lady Mary* (Waller) published in celebration of the wedding of the Duke of York's daughter. Waller writes a poem for the death of the Duke's month-old son (published 1682).

1678   Beginning of the Popish Plot, invented by Titus Oates and accomplices.

Proposal by Whigs to exclude the Catholic Duke of York from the succession (the 'Exclusion Crisis').

Garnet's Ghost (Oldham): pirated text of poem to be published later as the first of the *Satires upon the Jesuits*.

1679   January: King dissolves Parliament – Waller's last.

Duke of Monmouth (King's illegitimate son, and Whig candidate for the succession) makes a successful expedition against the Scots Covenanters; Waller writes a poem of praise, regretting that 'lampoons' have dishonoured Monmouth's achievement (published 1690).

A Satire against Virtue (Oldham), inspired by the figure of Lord Rochester (pirated text). Oldham leaves Croydon to be tutor to the grandson of Sir Edward Thurland at Reigate.

1680   Roscommon's translation of Horace's *Ars Poetica* published with a commendatory poem from Waller.

Rochester dies; Oldham writes an elegy (published 1681); Anne Wharton writes an elegy; Waller writes a poem of praise for her elegy (published 1690). Perhaps in this year Waller becomes acquainted with her and with her friend Bishop Burnet, who will describe him as 'a vain and empty, though a witty, man'.

Exclusion Bill defeated in the House of Lords.

1681   *Satires upon the Jesuits; Some New Pieces Never before Published* (Oldham) published. Probably in this year Oldham moves briefly to London and perhaps meets Dryden; then becomes tutor to the eldest son of Sir William Hicks at Low Leyton in Essex. Declines to accompany him abroad.

Dryden's satire *Absalom and Achitophel* published (a Tory response to the Exclusion Crisis).

1682   *Satires upon the Jesuits* (corrected edition) published.

Tories seize control of London; Whig leader Shaftesbury flees.

1683   *Poems and Translations* (Oldham) published.

Waller writes a poem in celebration of the Polish defeat of the Turks (published 1690)

December: Oldham dies of smallpox at the house of his new patron, the Earl of Kingston.

1684   *Remains of Mr John Oldham in Verse and Prose* published, with elegies, including one by Dryden.

1685   *Divine Poems* (Waller) published. Perhaps in this year, Waller buys a small house at Coleshill and becomes friendly there with the Quaker Thomas Ellwood, to whom he gives copies of his unpublished religious verse.

A Second Musical Entertainment performed on St Cecilia's Day (Oldham) published.

King dies. James II becomes King. Tactful warnings recorded in 1711 memoir from Waller, said to have predicted privately that the new King would be left 'like a whale upon the strand'.

1686 *Poems, etc.* (Waller) published – last edition.

Catholics appointed to the army and the courts, to strong popular displeasure.

1687 October: Waller dies of dropsy at Hall Barn. He is buried, in accordance with the recent law, in wool, not linen – an innovation he had attacked in Parliament. His will mentions seven daughters and four sons; it does not mention his second son, Edmund, whom the 1711 anonymous memoir names as his heir.

1688 December: Glorious Revolution: William of Orange enters London; James II flees to France.

1690 *The Maid's Tragedy Altered, with Some Other Pieces* and *The Second Part of Mr Waller's Poems* – two posthumous collections – published, the second with Preface probably by Bishop Atterbury, praising Waller as 'the parent of English verse, and the first that showed us our tongue had beauty and numbers in it'.

FURTHER READING

Critical works listed below include only fairly recent work, with a couple of classics that are easily obtainable in modern editions. Older views of Cowley are conveniently collected by Jean Loiseau in *Abraham Cowley's Reputation in England* (Paris, 1931) and Arthur H. Nethercot, 'The Reputation of Abraham Cowley (1660–1800)' *PMLA* 38 (1923), 588–641. Comments on Waller appear sparsely (often without references) in the introduction to Thorn Drury's edition, more fully in the unpublished Ph.D. dissertation by Margaret C. Deas (see below). Oldham criticism is summarized briefly in the Introduction to the Brooks and Selden edition.

COWLEY

Editions

[Sors Virgiliana] – British Library, London, Lansdowne MS 231, fol. 151
Poetical Blossoms (1633; 1636; 1637)
The Mistress (1647)
Poems (1656)
Verses Written upon Several Occasions (1663)
Thomas Sprat (ed.), *The Works of Mr Abraham Cowley* (1668; several subsequent editions)
Thomas Sprat (ed.), *Poemata Latina* (1668)
Allan Pritchard (ed.), *The Civil War* (Toronto, 1973)
Thomas O. Calhoun, Laurence Heyworth, et al. (eds.), *The Collected Works of Abraham Cowley* (Newark, DE, and London, 1989–: two volumes published so far)
David Hopkins and Tom Mason (eds.), *Abraham Cowley: Selected Poems* (Manchester, 1994)

Criticism

Samuel Johnson, 'Abraham Cowley' in *Lives of the English Poets* (many modern editions)

John McLaren McBryde Jr., 'A Study of Cowley's *Davideis*', *Journal of Germanic Philology* 2 (1899), 454–527

Arthur H. Nethercot, *Abraham Cowley: The Muse's Hannibal* (Oxford, 1931)

Jean Loiseau, *Abraham Cowley: Vie et Oeuvre* (Paris, 1931)

Robert B. Hinman, *Abraham Cowley's World of Order* (Cambridge, MA, 1960)

Maren-Sofie Røstvig, *The Happy Man: Studies in the Metamorphosis of a Classical Ideal*, vol. I: 1600–1700 (Oslo, revised edition, 1962)

Earl Miner, *The Metaphysical Mode from Donne to Cowley* (Princeton, NJ, 1969)

Penelope B. Wilson, 'The Knowledge and Appreciation of Pindar in the Seventeenth and Eighteenth Centuries', Oxford D.Phil, 1974

T. R. Langley, 'Abraham Cowley's "Brutus": Royalist or Republican?', *Yearbook of English Studies* 6 (1976), 41–52

David Trotter, *The Poetry of Abraham Cowley* (London, 1979)

Nicholas Jose, *Ideas of the Restoration in English Literature* (London, 1984)

Annabel M. Patterson, *Censorship and Interpretation: The Conditions of Writing and Reading in Early Modern England* (Madison, WI, 1984)

Anthony Low, *The Georgic Revolution* (Princeton, NJ, 1985)

Gerald F. MacLean, *Time's Witness: Historical Representation in English Poetry, 1603–1660* (Madison, WI, 1990)

Tom Mason, 'Abraham Cowley and the Wisdom of Anacreon', *Cambridge Quarterly* 19 (1990), 103–37

Stella P. Revard, 'Cowley's Anacreontiques and the Translation of the Greek Anacreontea' in Alexander Dalzell, Charles Fantazzi, Richard J. Schoeck (eds.), *Acta Conventus Neo-Latini Torontonensis* (Binghampton, NY, 1991)

Thomas N. Corns, *Uncloistered Virtue: English Political Literature 1640–1660* (Oxford, 1992)

Colin Burrow, *Epic Romance: Homer to Milton* (Oxford, 1993)

David Hopkins, 'Cowley's Horatian Mice' in Charles Martindale
 and David Hopkins (eds.), *Horace Made New* (Cambridge,
 1993)
Alastair Fowler, *The Country House Poem* (Edinburgh, 1994)

WALLER

Editions

[Sir John and Lady Denham] – University of Nottingham Library,
 MS Pw V 431
A Panegyric to my Lord Protector (1655; two versions)
A Poem on St. James's Park as lately improved by His Majesty
 (1661)
Instructions to a Painter for the Drawing of a Picture of the State and
 Posture of the English Forces at Sea, under the Command of his
 Royal Highness, in the Conclusion of the year 1664 (1665)
Upon Her Majesty's New Buildings at Somerset House (1665)
The New Masque for 'The Maid's Tragedy' (?1683)
Poems, etc. Written upon Several Occasions and to Several Persons
 (1645: several versions, all unauthorized; the best is the one
 'printed by I.N. for Hu[mphrey] Moseley'; 1664; 1668; 1682;
 1686)
The Maid's Tragedy Altered, with Some Other Pieces (1690)
The Second Part of Mr Waller's Poems (1690)
Poems, etc. [. . .] (1711): with anonymous memoir
Elijah Fenton (ed.), *The Works of Edmund Waller Esq. in Verse and*
 Prose (1729)
G. Thorn Drury (ed.), *The Poems of Edmund Waller* (1893; reprinted
 1901)

Criticism

Samuel Johnson, 'Edmund Waller' (see above)
Margaret C. Deas, 'A Study of the Life and Poetry of Edmund
 Waller', Cambridge diss., 1931
Alexander W. Allison, *Toward an Augustan Poetic: Edmund Waller's*
 'Reform' of English Poetry (Lexington, KY, 1962)

Ruth Nevo, *The Dial of Virtue: A Study of Poems on Affairs of State in the Seventeenth Century* (Princeton, NJ, 1963)

Joseph A. Mazzeo, 'Cromwell as Davidic King' in *Renaissance and Seventeenth-Century Studies* (New York and London, 1964)

Warren L. Chernaik, *The Poetry of Limitation: A Study of Edmund Waller* (New Haven and London, 1968)

Earl Miner, *The Cavalier Mode from Jonson to Cotton* (London, 1971)

Howard Erskine-Hill, *The Augustan Idea in English Literature* (London, 1983)

Nicholas Jose, *Ideas of the Restoration in English Literature* (see above)

Gerald Hammond, *Fleeting Things: English Poets and Poems 1616–1660* (Cambridge, MA, and London, 1990)

Geoffrey Hill, *The Enemy's Country: Words, Contexture, and Other Circumstances of Language* (Oxford, 1991)

Richard Hillyer, 'Better Read than Dead: Waller's "Of English Verse"', *Restoration* 14 (1990), 33–43

Steven N. Zwicker, *Lines of Authority: Politics and English Literary Culture, 1649–1689* (Ithaca, NY, 1994)

OLDHAM

Editions

Satires upon the Jesuits (1681; 1682)

Some New Pieces Never before Published (1681)

Poems and Translations (1683)

Remains of Mr John Oldham in Verse and Prose (1684)

A Second Musical Entertainment performed on St Cecilia's Day (1685)

The Works of Mr John Oldham, Together with his Remains (1722): with anonymous memoir

Harold F. Brooks and Raman Selden (eds.), *The Poems of John Oldham* (Oxford, 1987)

Criticism

Rachel Trickett, *The Honest Muse* (Oxford, 1967)

Emrys Jones, 'Pope and Dulness', *Proceedings of the British Academy*
    5 (1968), 231–63

David Wykes, 'Aspects of Restoration Irony: John Oldham', *English
    Studies* 52 (1971), 223–31

Harold F. Brooks, 'The Poems of John Oldham' in Harold A. Love
    (ed.), *Restoration Literature: Critical Approaches* (London,
    1972)

Raman Selden, 'Juvenal and Restoration Modes of Translation',
    Modern Language Review 68 (1972), 481–93

Howard Erskine-Hill, *The Augustan Idea in English Literature* (see
    above)

Paul Hammond, *John Oldham and the Renewal of Classical Culture*
    (Cambridge, 1983)

Raman Selden, 'The Young Marcellus of our Tongue: John Old-
    ham's Poetry', *Restoration* 9 (1985), 26–30

Raman Selden, 'Rochester and Oldham: "High Rants in Pro-
    faness"[sic]' *The Seventeenth Century* 6 (1991), 89–103

A NOTE ON THE TEXT

This text is based, for the most part, on the last version of each
poem published in the poet's lifetime or the first after his death.
For details, see Further Reading and Notes. In two cases, the text
used has been a modern edition: the extract from Cowley's *The
Civil War* is based on volume 1 of *The Collected Works of Abraham
Cowley* (1989); the extract from Oldham's fourth Jesuit satire is
based on the Brooks and Selden edition of *The Poems of John Oldham*
(1987).

Typography (italics and capitals), spelling and punctuation have
all been modified in line with modern usage. There are exceptions
to the last two.

Spelling is complicated by the question of elided syllables. There
are problems here with Cowley, who elides an unusual number.
Where the elision is helpful for the scansion and causes no confusion,
it is marked, for example, 'th'art' for 'the art', 'o'er' for 'over'.
Where the expanded form sounds no longer than the elided one in
modern verse, the elisions have been expanded (the ending -ed is
printed in the early texts as -'d unless the e is voiced; here the
expanded form is assumed to be silent, and the voiced -ed is
represented as -èd). The difficulty comes with elisions which are
necessary for the scansion but confusing to the reader when written
in elided form. I have encountered this problem only with Cowley,
who indicates such elisions in an idiosyncratic style by printing the
word complete, but with apostrophes; sometimes I have followed
his practice – for example, 'troubl'esome'. On the other hand, I
have tried to avoid the gasping effect of ubiquitous apostrophes.
The seventeenth-century texts are not entirely consistent about it,
and neither am I.

Punctuation is more delicate still. Seventeenth-century conven-
tions with commas and colons are different from the modern, and
need some altering in a modernized text; but repunctuating brings
to light ambiguities in the original which can only be bisected by

the change. None of the three poets seems to have bothered very much about it: in the errata slip to Cowley's 1656 volume, we find the blithe direction: 'false pointings [punctuation], false spellings, and such like venial faults . . . are recommended to [the reader's] judgement and candor to mend as he reads them'. Perhaps the most extreme example of dilemma is the end of Oldham's 'An Allusion to Martial . . .'. The 1683 text concludes like this:

> *The Price is much too dear*, you cry,
> *To give for both the Book, and me*:
> Yes doubtless, for such vanities,
> We know, Sir, you are too too wise.

The italics here represent Sir Tradewell's direct speech, and I have replaced them at the beginning with inverted commas; but 'me' in the second line refers to the poet ('you are not worth it' says the would-be borrower in the original Latin), so the inverted commas have to stop before the italics do. The poem is an epigram, which needs a snappy ending; to leave it in a muzz of ambiguity would be safe, but unsatisfactory. My solution is on p. 117, but it is only one possibility (the inverted commas could end after 'To give'). I have tried to respect the shape of the original sentences; readers who have the opportunity of looking at the early texts may like to compare their own decisions.

ABRAHAM COWLEY

from *A Vote*

This only grant me: that my means may lie
Too low for envy, for contempt too high.
   Some honour I would have
Not from great deeds but good alone:
Th' ignote are better than ill-known;
   Rumour can ope the grave.
Acquaintance I would hug, but when't depends
Not from the number but the choice of friends.

Books should, not business, entertain the light,
And sleep, as undisturbed as death, the night.
   My house a cottage, more
Than palace, and should fitting be
For all my use, no luxury;
   My garden painted o'er
With Nature's hand, not Art's, and pleasures yield
Horace might envy in his Sabine field.

Thus would I double my life's fading space,
For he that runs it well twice runs his race.
   And in this true delight,
These unbought sports and happy state,
I would not fear nor wish my fate,
   But boldly say each night,
'Tomorrow let my sun his beams display,
Or in clouds hide them; I have lived today.'

Against Fruition

No; thou'rt a fool, I'll swear, if e'er thou grant;
Much of my veneration thou must want
When once thy kindness puts my ignorance out,
For a learn'd age is always least devout.

Keep still thy distance, for at once to me
Goddess and woman too thou canst not be;
Thou'rt queen of all that sees thee, and as such
Must neither tyrannize nor yield too much;
Such freedoms give as may admit command,
10 But keep the forts and magazines in thine hand.
Thou'rt yet a whole world to me, and dost fill
My large ambition, but 'tis dangerous still,
Lest I like the Pellaean prince should be,
And weep for other worlds having conquered thee;
When Love has taken all thou hast away,
His strength by too much riches will decay.
Thou in my fancy dost much higher stand
Than women can be placed by Nature's hand,
And I must needs, I'm sure, a loser be
20 To change thee as thou'rt there, for very thee.
Thy sweetness is so much within me placed
That shouldst thou nectar give 'twould spoil the taste.
Beauty at first moves wonder and delight;
'Tis Nature's juggling trick to cheat the sight;
We'admire it whilst unknown, but after more
Admire ourselves for liking it before.
Love, like a greedy hawk, if we give way
Does over-gorge himself with his own prey;
Of very hopes a surfeit he'll sustain,
30 Unless by fears he cast them up again.
His spirit and sweetness dangers keep alone;
If once he lose his sting, he grows a drone.

The Heart-Breaking

It gave a piteous groan, and so it broke.
　　In vain it something would have spoke;
　　The love within too strong for't was,
Like poison put into a Venice glass.

I thought that this some remedy might prove;
   But oh, the mighty serpent Love,
   Cut by this chance in pieces small,
In all still lived and still it stung in all.

And now, alas, each little broken part
10   Feels the whole pain of all my heart;
   And every smallest corner still
Lives with that torment which the whole did kill.

Even so rude armies, when the field they quit
   And into several quarters get,
   Each troop does spoil and ruin more
Than all joined in one body did before.

How many loves reign in my bosom now?
   How many loves, yet all of you?
   Thus have I changed, with evil fate,
20 My monarch-love into a tyrant-state.

The Motto

Tentanda via est, &c.

What shall I do to be for ever known,
   And make the age to come my own?
I shall like beasts or common people die
   Unless you write my elegy;
Whilst others, great by being born are grown,
   Their mothers' labour, not their own.
In this scale gold, in the other fame does lie;
   The weight of that, mounts this so high.
These men are Fortune's jewels, moulded bright,
10   Brought forth with their own fire and light;
If I, her vulgar stone, for either look
   Out of myself it must be strook.

Yet I must on; what sound is't strikes mine ear?
    Sure I Fame's trumpet hear.
It sounds like the Last Trumpet, for it can
    Raise up the buried man.
Unpassed Alps stop me, but I'll cut through all,
    And march, the Muse's Hannibal.
Hence, all the flattering vanities that lay
20   Nets of roses in the way;
Hence, the desire of honours, or estate,
    And all that is not above Fate;
Hence, Love himself, that tyrant of my days,
    Which intercepts my coming praise.
Come, my best friends, my books, and lead me on;
    'Tis time that I were gone.
Welcome, great Stagyrite, and teach me now
    All I was born to know.
Thy scholar's victries thou dost far outdo:
30   He conquered th' Earth, the whole World you.
Welcome, learn'd Cicero, whose blest tongue and wit
    Preserves Rome's greatness yet.
Thou art the first of orators; only he
    Who best can praise thee, next must be.
Welcome, the Mantuan Swan, Virgil the wise,
    Whose verse walks highest but not flies;
Who brought green poesy to her perfect age
    And made that art which was a rage.
Tell me, ye mighty three, what shall I do
40   To be like one of you?
But you have climbed the mountain's top, there sit
    On the calm flourishing head of it;
And whilst with wearied steps we upward go,
    See us, and clouds, below.

On the Death of Sir Anthony Van Dyck
The famous Painter

Van Dyck is dead; but what bold Muse shall dare
(Though poets in that word with painters share)
T'express her sadness? Poesy must become
An art like painting here, an art that's dumb.
Let's all our solemn grief in silence keep,
Like some sad picture which he made to weep,
Or those who saw't; for none his works could view
Unmoved with the same passions which he drew.
His pieces so with their live objects strive
10   That both, or pictures seem, or both alive.
Nature herself, amazed, does doubting stand
Which is her own and which the painter's hand,
And does attempt the like with less success
When her own work in twins she would express.
His all-resembling pencil did out-pass
The mimic imagery of looking-glass;
Nor was his life less perfect than his art,
Nor was his hand less erring than his heart.
There was no false or fading colour there;
20   The figures sweet and well proportioned were.
Most other men, set next to him in view,
Appeared more shadows than the men he drew.
Thus still he lived till Heav'n did for him call,
Where reverend Luke salutes him first of all;
Where he beholds new sights, divinely fair,
And could almost wish for his pencil there,
Did he not gladly see how all things shine,
Wondrously painted in the Mind Divine;
Whilst he, forever ravished with the show,
30   Scorns his own art which we admire below.
   Only his beauteous lady still he loves
(The love of heav'nly objects Heav'n improves);
He sees bright angels in pure beams appear,
And thinks on her he left so like them here.

And you, fair widow, who stay here alive,
Since he so much rejoices, cease to grieve.
Your joys and griefs were wont the same to be;
Begin not now, blest pair, to disagree.
No wonder death moved not his genrous mind;
40   You, and a new-born you, he left behind.
Even Fate expressed his love to his dear wife,
And let him end your picture with his life.

THE CIVIL WAR

from *Book II [The Devil Speaks]*

'Tis only peace breeds scarcity in Hell.
Which that the Stygian tyrant might prevent,
He calls below a dreadful parliament.
Deep in a dismal den, Belzebub's Hall,
The fiends all meet at their grim Sovereign's call.
From every part of that wide land they come;
The souls awhile rest from their endless doom.
They rest awhile; but woe to man above!
For none but mighty ill these sessions move:
10   The change of a religion or a state,
Mischiefs of greatest consequence and weight.
Th' affairs of bleeding Britain called them now;
Alas, unhappy isle, what wilt thou do!
They all set round, and from his direful throne
Of burnished flames the Tyrant rose alone.
Much anger in his words, much in his look;
The fiends themselves and all Hell's empire shook.
      'My friends and fellow gods:
I need not, I suppose, the desperate state
20   Of all our British hopes to you relate.
You've heard and seen 't and are ashamed, I know,
To see our bold confederates fall'n so low,
Since coward Fiennes did from lost Bristol flee,
Against those solemn oaths to 's God and me.
Which, shall we'endure? Shall we sit tame and still,
Suffering a cause so'unjust to thrive so ill?
Shall we behold long, sleepy peace again,
The ill of Charles's dull and godly reign?
Shall we again the bishops' pride behold
30   Which sixteen hundred years hath us controlled?
It must not be; by my great self, I swear
Had I another Heav'n I'd venture 't here;

The cause is ours, ours the chief gain will be;
Is Saye or Pym concerned so much as we?
Go then, haste all to Lud's seditious town;
Ye know and love 't; scarce Hell is more your own.
There's nothing now your great design to stay;
God and his troubl'esome spirits are gone away.'
I heard the voice, I heard it bid them go;
40   'Twas a good sound! They left Jerus'alem so!
Seek first the men who our high business sway:
St Johns, the Vanes, Kimbolton, Pym, and Saye.
Without a noise possess their souls; get in
As subtly as the close Original Sin
Seizes the new-formed infant in the womb,
And let your acts show first that you are come.
Urge their loud fears, unmask their ugly guilt;
Too shallow's yet the stream of blood they've spilt;
Tell them they all on dangerous rocks are cast,
50   And some high tide must bring them off at last.
Bid them rush on, break through all sins their way;
Vengeance behind o'ertakes them if they stay.
With such bold deeds let them the world amaze
That men shall find no leisure to dispraise.
Tell them what mighty names they're like to grow,
Whilst modest Catiline blushes here below;
With shame and envy their high acts he sees,
And seems a Cicero when compared with these.
Tell them how brave a funeral they may have,
60   They and three kingdoms with them in one grave,
When they shall say to Fate, 'You owe us more
Than all your famines and sick years before;'
When each shall public ruin round him see,
And, as he falls, cry out, ''Twas done by me.'
Their gallant deeds, my friends, will ours excel;
We, we ourselves from Heav'n less nobly fell.
This at the worst; then brighter things suggest:
All the bold hopes that swell a traitor's breast;
Conquest with slaughter (else 'twill make no show);
70   The Crown cast down to earth, the King more low;

The Church's lands (alas, what's that? 'tis less
Than will suffice their very wantonness,
Much less their avarice); all the kingdom's wealth,
Theirs, not, as now, by borrowing, plunder, stealth,
But openly confessed and by a law;
For such shall votes be then and such their awe.
Th'estates and lives shall be their own, of all
Whom they by'unpopular names but please to call;
Their rage and furious avarice shall appear,
80   Boundless as Marius' sword and Sulla's spear.
If in their misty souls there chance to shine
The smallest peaceful glimpse of light divine,
Raise up new fogs and thicken clouds apace,
Till all our night of Hell confuse the place.
Next, to their priests: use here all art and care;
Be you to them what they to th'people are.
Their sordid souls with dull rewards enflame,
Large feasts, and larger gifts, and popular fame.
But sometimes shake the halter and the chain;
90   Show them their islands and New World again.
Bid them now groan and knock the pulpit more,
Pray longer, and preach louder, than before;
Bid them renew old blasphemies and fling
All texts of wicked princes at their King;
Bid them their mouth-granadoes cast about,
Till their own fires seize all the catching rout.
Then into every street your force divide;
Swarm like the plagues that scourged old Pharaoh's pride;
Men's breasts with thirst of blood and fury fill;
100   Spare not, for 'twill be thought God's Spirit still.
Strengthen weak rebels and confirm the bold;
Add fuel to the hot, flame to the cold.
In different shapes to differing minds appear,
In shapes of hope and zeal and hate and fear.
Learn this wise art from your grand en'emy, Paul,
And to gain some, do you turn all to all.
Pluck from their hearts each mild and sober thought,
Till war and public woe with joy be bought

Ev'n by the covetous; till pale cowards fight,
110   And all men crowd to ruin with delight.
Cease not, my friends, till you their ensigns spy
Advanced 'gainst Charles's army and the sky.
The rest, when once their banners spread ye see,
Leave to th'eternal Justice, and to me.

[Sors Virgiliana]

By a bold people's stubborn arms oppressed,
Forced to forsake the land he once possessed,
Torn from his dearest son, let him in vain
Seek help, and see his friends unjustly slain;
Let him to base, unequal terms submit
In hopes to save his crown, yet lose both it
And life at once; untimely let him die,
And on an open stage unburied lie.

On the Death of Mr Crashaw

Poet and saint! To thee alone are given
The two most sacred names of earth and Heaven;
The hard and rarest union which can be,
Next that of Godhead with humanity.
Long did the Muses banished slaves abide,
And built vain pyramids to mortal pride;
Like Moses, thou (though spells and charms withstand)
Hast brought them nobly home back to their Holy Land.
   Ah wretched we, poets of earth! But thou
10   Wert, living, the same poet which thou'rt now,
Whilst angels sing to thee their airs divine,
And joy in an applause so great as thine.
Equal society with them to hold,
Thou need'st not make new songs but say the old.
And they (kind spirits!) shall all rejoice to see
How little less then they exalted man may be.
Still the old heathen gods in numbers dwell;
The heav'nliest thing on earth still keeps up Hell.
Nor have we yet quite purged the Christian land:
20   Still idols here, like calves at Bethel, stand;
And though Pan's death long since all oracles breaks,
Yet still in rhyme the fiend Apollo speaks.

Nay, with the worst of heathen dotage, we
(Vain men!) the monster Woman deify;
Find stars, and tie our fates there, in a face,
And Paradise in them by whom we lost it place.
What different faults corrupt our Muses thus?
Wanton as girls, as old wives fabulous!
    Thy spotless Muse, like Mary, did contain
30 The boundless Godhead; she did well disdain
That her eternal verse employed should be
On a less subject then Eternity;
And for a sacred mistress scorned to take
But her whom God himself scorned not his spouse to make.
It, in a kind, her miracle did do:
A fruitful mother was, and virgin too.
    How well, blest swan, did Fate contrive thy death,
And made thee render up thy tuneful breath
In thy great mistress' arms! Thou most divine
40 And richest offering of Loretto's shrine,
Where, like some holy sacrifice t'expire,
A fever burns thee and Love lights the fire!
Angels, they say, brought the famed chapel there,
And bore the sacred load in triumph through the air;
'Tis surer much they brought thee there, and they,
And thou, their charge, went singing all the way.
    Pardon, my Mother Church, if I consent
That angels led him when from thee he went;
For even error sure no danger is
50 When joined with so much piety as his.
Ah, mighty God, with shame I speak 't and grief,
Ah, that our greatest faults were in belief,
And our weak reason were ev'n weaker yet,
Rather than thus our wills too strong for it!
His faith perhaps in some nice tenets might
Be wrong; his life, I'm sure, was in the right;
And I myself a Catholic will be,
So far at least, great saint, to pray to thee.
    Hail, Bard Triumphant, and some care bestow
60 On us, the Poets Militant below!

Opposed by our old enemy, adverse Chance,
Attacked by Envy and by Ignorance,
Enchained by Beauty, tortured by Desires,
Exposed by tyrant Love to savage beasts and fires.
Thou from low Earth in nobler flames didst rise,
And, like Elijah, mount alive the skies.
Elisha-like (but with a wish much less,
More fit thy greatness and my littleness),
Lo, here I beg (I whom thou once didst prove
70   So humble to esteem, so good to love),
Not that thy spirit might on me doubled be;
I ask but half thy mighty spirit for me;
And when my Muse soars with so strong a wing,
'Twill learn of things divine, and first of thee, to sing.

ANACREONTICS

II Drinking

The thirsty earth soaks up the rain,
And drinks, and gapes for drink again.
The plants suck in the earth, and are
With constant drinking fresh and fair.
The sea itself, which one would think
Should have but little need of drink,
Drinks ten thousand rivers up,
So filled that they o'erflow the cup.
The busy sun (and one guess
By 's drunken fiery face no less)
Drinks up the sea, and when he's done,
The moon and stars drink up the sun.
They drink and dance by their own light;
They drink and revel all the night.
Nothing in Nature's sober found,
But an eternal health goes round.
Fill up the bowl then, fill it high,
Fill all the glasses there, for why
Should every creature drink but I –
Why, Man of Morals, tell me why?

V Age

Oft am I by the women told,
'Poor Anacreon, thou grow'st old.
Look how thy hairs are falling all;
Poor Anacreon, how they fall!'
Whether I grow old or no,
By th'effects I do not know.

This I know without being told,
'Tis time to live if I grow old;
'Tis time short pleasures now to take,
Of little life the best to make,
And manage wisely the last stake.

X The Grasshopper

Happy insect, what can be
In happiness compared to thee?
Fed with nourishment divine,
The dewy morning's gentle wine!
Nature waits upon thee still,
And thy verdant cup does fill;
'Tis filled where ever thou dost tread;
Nature's self's thy Ganymed.
Thou dost drink and dance and sing,
Happier than the happiest king!
All the fields which thou dost see,
All the plants belong to thee;
All that summer hours produce,
Fertile made with early juice.
Man for thee does sow and plough;
Farmer he, and landlord thou!
Thou dost innocently joy,
Nor does thy luxury destroy;
The shepherd gladly heareth thee,
More harmonious than he.
Thee country hinds with gladness hear,
Prophet of the ripened year!
Thee Phoebus loves and does inspire;
Phoebus is himself thy sire.
To thee, of all things upon earth,
Life is no longer than thy mirth.
Happy insect, happy thou,
Dost neither age nor winter know.

But when thou'st drunk and danced and sung
30 Thy fill, the flowery leaves among
(Voluptuous, and wise withal,
Epicurean animal!),
Sated with thy summer feast,
Thou retir'st to endless rest.

Brutus

Excellent Brutus, of all human race
The best till Nature was improved by Grace;
Till men above themselves Faith raisèd more
    Than Reason above beasts before!
Virtue was thy life's centre, and from thence
Did silently and constantly dispense
    The gentle vigorous influence
To all the wide and fair circumference;
And all the parts upon it leaned so easily,
Obeyed the mighty force so willingly,
That none could discord or disorder see
    In all their contrariety.
Each had his motion, natural and free,
And the whole no more moved than the whole world could
      be.

From thy strict rule some think that thou didst swerve
(Mistaken honest men!) in Caesar's blood;
What mercy could the Tyrant's life deserve
From him who killed himself rather than serve?
Th' heroic exaltations of Good
    Are so far from understood
We count them vice; alas, our sight's so ill
That things which swiftest move seem to stand still.
We look not upon Virtue in her height,
On her supreme idea, brave and bright
    In the original light,
  But as her beams reflected pass
Through our own nature or ill custom's glass.
    And 'tis no wonder so,
    If with dejected eye
    In standing pools we seek the sky,
That stars so high above should seem to us below.

   Can we stand by and see
Our mother robbed and bound and ravished be,
      Yet not to her assistance stir,
Pleased with the strength and beauty of the ravisher?
Or shall we fear to kill him, if before
      The cancelled name of Friend he bore?
   Ingrateful Brutus do they call?
Ingrateful Caesar who could Rome enthrall!
40 An act more barbarous and unnatural
(In th'exact balance of true Virtue tried)
Than his successor Nero's parricide!
   There's none but Brutus could deserve
   That all men else should wish to serve,
And Caesar's usurped place to him should proffer;
None can deserve't but he who would refuse the offer.

   Ill Fate assumed a body thee t'affright,
And wrapped itself i'th'terrors of the night.
'I'll meet thee at Philippi,' said the Sprite;
50   'I'll meet thee there,' saidst thou,
   With such a voice and such a brow
As put the trembling ghost to sudden flight.
      It vanished, as a taper's light
      Goes out when spirits appear in sight.
One would have thought 't had heard the morning crow,
   Or seen her well-appointed star
Come marching up the eastern hill afar;
Nor durst it in Philippi's field appear,
   But unseen attacked thee there.
60 Had it presumed in any shape thee to oppose,
Thou wouldst have forced it back upon thy foes,
      Or slain 't like Caesar, though it be
A conqueror and a monarch mightier far than he.

What joy can human things to us afford
When we see perish thus by odd events,
   Ill men, and wretched accidents,
The best cause and best man that ever drew a sword?

> When we see
The false Octavius and wild Antony,
70   God-like Brutus, conquer thee?
What can we say but thine own tragic word,
That Virtue, which had worshipped been by thee
As the most solid good and greatest deity,
     By this fatal proof became
     An idol only and a name.
  Hold, noble Brutus, and restrain
The bold voice of thy generous disdain;
     These mighty gulfs are yet
Too deep for all thy judgment and thy wit.
80 The time's set forth already which shall quell
Stiff Reason when it offers to rebel;
     Which these great secrets shall unseal,
     And new philosophies reveal.
A few years more, so soon hadst thou not died,
Would have confounded Human Virtue's pride,
     And showed thee a God crucified.

To Mr Hobbes

  Vast bodies of philosophy
    I oft have seen and read,
    But all are bodies dead,
  Or bodies by art fashionèd;
I never yet the living soul could see,
    But in thy books and thee.
  'Tis only God can know
Whether the fair idea thou dost show
Agree entirely with his own or no;
10   This I dare boldly tell,
'Tis so like truth 'twill serve our turn as well.
Just, as in Nature, thy proportions be,
As full of concord their variety,

As firm the parts upon their centre rest,
And all so solid are that they, at least
As much as Nature, emptiness detest.

Long did the mighty Stagyrite retain
The universal intellectual reign;
Saw his own country's short-lived leopard slain;
20   The stronger Roman eagle did outfly,
Oftener renewed his age, and saw that die;
Mecca itself, in spite of Máhomet, possessed,
And, chased by a wild deluge from the east,
His monarchy new planted in the west.
But as in time each great imperial race
Degenerates and gives some new one place,
        So did this noble empire waste,
        Sunk by degrees from glories past,
And in the schoolmen's hands it perished quite at last.
30   Then nought but words it grew,
          And those all barbarous too.
      It perished and it vanished there;
The life and soul, breathed out, became but empty air.

The fields which answered well the ancients' plough,
Spent and outworn, return no harvest now;
In barren age, wild and unglorious lie,
        And boast of past fertility,
The poor relief of present poverty.
      Food and fruit we now must want
40   Unless new lands we plant.
We break up tombs with sacrilegious hands;
        Old rubbish we remove;
To walk in ruins, like vain ghosts, we love,
      And with fond divining wánds
        We search among the dead
        For treasures burièd,
      Whilst still the liberal Earth does hold
So many virgin mines of undiscovered gold.

The Baltic, Euxine, and the Caspian,
50   And slender-limbed Mediterranean,
Seem narrow creeks to thee, and only fit
For the poor wretched fisher-boats of Wit.
Thy nobler vessel the vast ocean tries,
          And nothing sees but seas and skies
          Till unknown regions it descries,
Thou great Columbus of the golden lands of new
          philosophies!
          Thy task was harder much then his,
          For thy learn'd America is
          Not only found out first by thee
60   And rudely left to future industry,
          But thy eloquence and thy Wit
Has planted, peopled, built, and civ'ilized it.

          I little thought before
          (Nor, being my own self so poor,
          Could comprehend so vast a store)
     That all the wardrobe of rich eloquence
          Could have afforded half enough
          Of bright, of new, and lasting stuff
To clothe the mighty limbs of thy gigantic sense.
70   Thy solid reason, like the shield from Heaven
          To the Trojan hero given,
Too strong to take a mark from any mortal dart,
Yet shines with gold and gems in every part,
And wonders on it 'graved by the learn'd hand of Art;
          A shield that gives delight
          Ev'n to the enemies' sight,
Then, when they're sure to lose the combat by't.

Nor can the snow, which now cold Age does shed
          Upon thy reverend head,
80   Quench or allay the noble fires within;
          But all which thou hast been,
          And all that youth can be, thou'rt yet,
          So fully still dost thou

Enjoy the manhood and the bloom of Wit
And all the natural heat, but not the fever too.
So contraries on Etna's top conspire;
Here hoary frosts and by them breaks out fire.
A secure peace the faithful neighbours keep;
Th'emboldened snow next to the flame does sleep.
90   And if we weigh, like thee,
          Nature and causes, we shall see
          That thus it needs must be;
To things immortal, Time can do no wrong,
And that which never is to die, forever must be young.

The Muse

Go, the rich chariot instantly prepare;
    The Queen, my Muse, will take the air.
Unruly Fancy with strong Judgment trace,
    Put in nimble-footed Wit,
    Smooth-paced Eloquence join with it,
Sound Memory with young Invention place,
    Harness all the wingèd race.
Let the postillion Nature mount and let
    The coachman Art be set,
10 And let the airy footmen running all beside
    Make a long row of goodly pride.
Figures, Conceits, Raptures, and Sentences
        In a well-worded dress;
And innocent Loves and pleasant Truths and useful Lies,
        In all their gaudy liveries.
    Mount, glorious Queen, thy travelling throne,
        And bid it to put on;
    For long, though cheerful, is the way,
And life, alas, allows but one ill winter's day.

20   Where never foot of man or hoof of beast
          The passage pressed;
      Where never fish did fly,
And with short, silver wings cut the low, liquid sky;
      Where bird with painted oars did ne'er
Row through the trackless ocean of the air;
          Where never yet did pry
      The busy morning's curious eye,
The wheels of thy bold coach pass quick and free,
      And all's an open road to thee.
30   Whatever God did say
Is all thy plain and smooth, uninterrupted way.
Nay, ev'n beyond his works thy voyages are known:
      Thou 'st thousand worlds too of thine own.
Thou speak'st, great Queen, in the same style as he,
And a new world leaps forth when thou say'st, 'Let it be.'

Thou fathom'st the deep gulf of ages past,
      And canst pluck up with ease
The years which thou dost please,
Like shipwracked treasures by rude tempests cast
40   Long since into the sea,
Brought up again to light and public use by thee.
      Nor dost thou only dive so low,
          But fly
With an unwearied wing the other way on high
      Where Fates among the stars do grow;
There into the close nests of Time dost peep,
          And there with piercing eye
Through the firm shell and the thick white dost spy
          Years to come a-forming lie,
50   Close in their sacred secondine asleep,
          Till, hatched by the sun's vital heat
          Which o'er them yet does brooding set,
          They life and motion get,
      And, ripe at last with vigorous might,
Break through the shell and take their everlasting flight.

And sure we may
The same too of the present say,
If past and future times do thee obey.
Thou stop'st this current, and dost make
60   This running river settle like a lake;
Thy certain hand holds fast this slippery snake.
The fruit which does so quickly waste
Men scarce can see it, much less taste,
Thou comfitest in sweets to make it last.
This shining piece of ice,
Which melts so soon away
With the sun's ray,
Thy verse does solidate and crystallize
Till it a lasting mirror be.
70   Nay, thy immortal rhyme
Makes this one short point of Time
To fill up half the orb of round Eternity.

DAVIDEIS

from *Book: I [Music]*

Tell me, O Muse (for thou or none canst tell
The mystic pow'rs that in blest numbers dwell;
Thou their great nature know'st, nor is it fit
This noblest gem of thine own crown t'omit):
Tell me from whence these heav'nly charms arise;
Teach the dull world t'admire what they despise.
  As first a various, unformed hint we find
Rise in some godlike poet's fertile mind,
Till all the parts and words their places take,
10 And, with just marches, verse and music make;
Such was God's poem, this world's new essay;
So wild and rude in its first draught it lay;
Th'ungoverned parts no correspondence knew,
An artless war from thwarting motions grew,
Till they to number and fixed rules were brought
By the eternal Mind's poetic thought.
Water and air he for the tenor chose;
Earth made the bass, the treble, flame arose;
To th' active moon a quick, brisk stroke he gave;
20 To Saturn's string a touch more soft and grave.
The motions, straight and round and swift and slow
And short and long, were mixed and woven so,
Did in such artful figures smoothly fall,
As made this decent, measured dance of all.
And this is Music; sounds that charm our ears
Are but one dressing that rich science wears.
Though no man hear't, though no man it rehearse,
Yet will there still be music in my verse.
In this great world so much of it we see;
30 The lesser, Man, is all–o'er harmony.
Storehouse of all proportions! Single choir,
Which first God's breath did tunefully inspire!

From hence blest Music's heav'nly charms arise,
From sympathy which them and man allies.
Thus they our souls, thus they our bodies win:
Not by their force, but party that's within.
Thus the strange cure, on our spilt blood applied,
Sympathy to the distant wound does guide.
Thus when two brethren strings are set alike,
40   To move them both but one of them we strike.
Thus David's lyre did Saul's wild rage control,
And tuned the harsh disorders of his soul.

from *Book III [Lot's Wife]*

Behind his wife stood, ever fixed alone;
No more a woman, not yet quite a stone.
A lasting death seized on her turning head;
One cheek was rough and white, the other red
And yet a cheek; in vain to speak she strove;
Her lips, though stone, a little seemed to move.
One eye was closed, surprised by sudden night;
The other trembled still with parting light.
The wind admired, which her hair loosely bore,
10   Why it grew stiff and now would play no more.
To Heav'n she lifted up her freezing hands,
And to this day a suppliant pillar stands.
She tried her heavy foot from ground to rear,
And raised the heel, but her toe's rooted there.
Ah, foolish woman, who must always be
A sight more strange than that she turned to see!

On the Queen's Repairing Somerset House

When God (the cause to me and men unknown)
Forsook the royal houses and his own,
And both abandoned to the common foe,
How near to ruin did my glories go?
Nothing remained t' adorn this princely place
Which covetous hands could take or rude deface.
In all my rooms and galleries, I found
The richest figures torn, and all around
Dismembered statues of great heroes lay;
10   Such Naseby's field seemed on the fatal day.
And me, when nought for robbery was left,
They starved to death; the gasping walls were cleft,
The pillars sunk, the roofs above me wept;
No sign of spring or joy my garden kept;
Nothing was seen which could content the eye,
Till dead the impious tyrant here did lie.
   See how my face is changed, and what I am
Since my true mistress, and now foundress, came.
It does not fill her bounty to restore
20   Me as I was (nor was I small) before:
She imitates the kindness to her shown;
She does, like Heav'n (which the dejected throne
At once restores, fixes, and higher rears),
Strengthen, enlarge, exalt what she repairs.
And now I dare (though proud I must not be,
Whilst my great Mistress I so humbly see
In all her various glories): now I dare
Ev'n with the proudest palaces compare;
My beauty and convenience will, I'm sure,
30   So just a boast with modesty endure;
And all must to me yield when I shall tell
How I am placed and who does in me dwell.
   Before my gate a street's broad channel goes,
Which still with waves of crowding people flows;
And every day there passes by my side,
Up to its western reach, the London tide,

The spring-tides of the term; my front looks down
On all the pride and business of the town.
My other front (for as in kings we see
40   The liveliest image of the deity,
We in their houses should Heav'n's likeness find,
Where nothing can be said to be behind),
My other fair and more majestic face
(Who can the fair to more advantage place?)
For ever gazes on itself below
In the best mirror that the world can show.

    And here, behold, in a long, bending row,
How two joint cities make one glorious bow;
The midst, the noblest place, possessed by me;
50   Best to be seen by all, and all o'ersee.
Which way soe'er I turn my joyful eye,
Here the great Court, there the rich Town I spy;
On either side dwells safety and delight;
Wealth on the left and power upon the right.
T' assure yet my defence, on either hand,
Like, mighty forts in equal distance stand;
Two of the best and stateliest piles which e'er
Man's liberal piety of old did rear,
Where the two princes of th' apostles' band,
60   My neighbours and my guards, watch and command.

    My warlike guard of ships, which farther lie,
Might be my object too, were not the eye
Stopped by the houses of that wondrous street
Which rides o'er the broad river like a fleet.
The stream's eternal siege they, fixed, abide,
And the swoll'n stream's auxiliary tide;
Though both their ruin with joint power conspire,
Both to outbrave, they nothing dread but fire.
And here my Thames, though it more gentle be
70   Than any flood so strengthened by the sea,
Finding by art his natural forces broke,
And bearing, captive-like, the archèd yoke,
Does roar and foam and rage at the disgrace,
But recomposes straight and calms his face,

Is into reverence and submission strook,
As soon as from afar he does but look
Tow'rds the white palace where that King does reign
Who lays his laws and bridges o'er the main.
    Amidst these louder honours of my seat,
80 And two vast cities, troublesomely great,
In a large, various plain the country too
Opens her gentler blessings to my view;
In me the active and the quiet mind
By different ways equal content may find.
If any prouder virtuoso's sense
At that part of my prospect take offence
By which the meaner cabanes are descried
Of my imperial river's humbler side:
If they call that a blemish, let them know
90 God, and my godlike Mistress, think not so;
For the distressed and the afflicted lie
Most in their care and always in their eye.
    And thou, fair River, who still pay'st to me
Just homage in thy passage to the sea,
Take here this one instruction as thou go'st:
When thy mixed waves shall visit every coast,
When round the world their voyage they shall make,
And back to thee some secret channels take,
Ask them what nobler sight they e'er did meet
100 Except thy mighty Master's sovereign fleet,
Which now trimphant o'er the main does ride,
The terror of all lands, the ocean's pride.
    From hence his kingdoms, happy now at last,
(Happy, if wise by their misfortunes past);
From hence may omens take of that success
Which both their future wars and peace shall bless:
The peaceful mother on mild Thames does build;
With her son's fabrics the rough sea is filled.

The Complaint

In a deep vision's intellectual scene,
    Beneath a bower for sorrow made,
        Th' uncomfortable shade
    Of the black yew's unlucky green
Mixed with the mourning willow's careful grey,
Where reverend Cam cuts out his famous way,
    The melancholy Cowley lay;
And lo, a Muse appeared to 's closèd sight
(The Muses oft in lands of vision play),
Bodied, arrayed, and seen by an internal light.
A golden harp with silver strings she bore;
A wondrous hieroglyphic robe she wore,
That Nature or that Fancy can create,
    That Art can never imitate,
And with loose pride it wantoned in the air.
In such a dress, in such a well-clothed dream,
She used of old, near fair Ismenus' stream,
Pindar, her Theban favourite, to meet;
A crown was on her head and wings were on her feet.

She touched him with her harp and raised him from the
        ground;
The shaken strings melodiously resound.
    'Art thou returned at last,' said she,
    'To this forsaken place and me?
Thou prodigal, who didst so loosely waste
Of all thy youthful years the good estate;
Art thou returned here to repent too late
And gather husks of learning up at last,
Now the rich harvest time of life is past
    And winter marches on so fast?
But when I meant t' adopt thee for my son,
And did as learn'd a portion assign
As ever any of the mighty Nine
    Had to their dearest children done;

10

20

30

When I resolved t' exalt thy anointed name
Among the spiritual lords of peaceful fame,
Thou changeling, thou, bewitched with noise and show,
Wouldst into courts and cities from me go;
Wouldst see the world abroad and have a share
In all the follies and the tumults there!
40   Thou wouldst, forsooth, be something in a state,
And business thou wouldst find and wouldst create:
   Business, the frivolous pretence
Of human lusts to shake off innocence!
   Business, the grave impertinence!
Business, the thing which I of all things hate!
Business, the contradiction of thy fate!

'Go, renegado, cast up thy account,
     And see to what amount
   Thy foolish gains by quitting me:
50   The sale of knowledge, fame, and liberty,
The fruits of thy unlearn'd apostasy.
Thou thought'st if once the public storm were past,
All thy remaining life should sunshine be;
Behold, the public storm is spent at last;
The Sovereign is tossed at sea no more,
And thou, with all the noble company,
     Art got at last to shore.
But whilst thy fellow-voyagers I see
All marched up to possess the promised land,
60   Thou still alone, alas, dost gaping stand,
Upon the naked beach, upon the barren sand.

'As a fair morning of the blessed spring
   After a tedious, stormy night,
Such was the glorious entry of our King;
Enriching moisture dropped on everything;
Plenty he sowed below and cast about him light.
   But then, alas, to thee alone
One of old Gideon's miracles was shown;

For every tree and every herb around
70   With pearly dew was crowned,
And upon all the quickened ground
The fruitful seed of Heav'n did brooding lie,
And nothing but the Muses' fleece was dry.
    It did all other threats surpass,
When God to his own people said
(The men whom through long wanderings he had led)
    That he would give them ev'n a Heav'n of brass;
They looked up to that Heav'n in vain,
That bounteous Heav'n, which God did not restrain
80   Upon the most unjust to shine and rain.

'The Rachel, for which twice seven years and more
    Thou didst with faith and labour serve
And didst (if faith and labour can) deserve,
    Though she contracted was to thee,
Giv'n to another thou didst see;
    Giv'n to another, who had store
Of fairer and of richer wives before;
And not a Leah left, thy recompense to be.
Go on, twice seven years more thy fortune try;
90   Twice seven years more God in his bounty may
        Give thee, to fling away
Into the Court's deceitful lottery.
    But think how likely 'tis that thou,
With the dull work of thy unwieldy plough,
Shouldst in a hard and barren season thrive –
    Shouldst even able be to live;
Thou, to whose share so little bread did fall
In the miraculous year when manna rained on all.'

Thus spake the Muse, and spake it with a smile
100   That seemed at once to pity and revile.
And to her thus, raising his thoughtful head,
    The melancholy Cowley said:
    'Ah, wanton foe, dost thou upbraid
    The ills which thou thyself hast made?

When in the cradle, innocent, I lay,
Thou, wicked spirit, stolest me away,
    And my abusèd soul didst bear
Into thy new-found worlds, I know not where,
    Thy golden Indies in the air;
110   And ever since I strive in vain
    My ravished freedom to regain;
    Still I rebel, still thou dost reign;
Lo, still in verse against thee I complain.
    There is a sort of stubborn weeds
Which if the earth but once, it ever breeds.
    No wholesome herb can near them thrive;
    No useful plant can keep alive.
The foolish sports I did on thee bestow
Make all my art and labour fruitless now;
120 Where once such fairies dance, no grass doth ever grow.

'When my new mind had no infusion known,
Thou gav'st so deep a tincture of thine own
    That ever since I vainly try
    To wash away th' inherent dye;
Long work perhaps may spoil thy colours quite,
But never will reduce the native white;
    To all the ports of honour and of gain
    I often steer my course, in vain;
Thy gale comes 'cross, and drives me back again.
130 Thou slack'nest all my nerves of industry
    By making them so oft to be
The tinkling strings of thy loose minstrelsy.
Whoever this world's happiness would see
    Must as entirely cast off thee
    As they who only Heav'n desire
      Do from the world retire.
This was my error, this my gross mistake,
Myself a demi-votary to make.
Thus, with Sapphira and her husband's fate
140 (A fault which I, like them, am taught too late),
For all that I gave up I nothing gain,
And perish for the part which I retain.

'Teach me not then, O thou fallacious Muse,
    The Court and better King t' accuse;
The Heaven under which I live is fair;
The fertile soil will a full harvest bear;
Thine, thine is all the barrenness, if thou
Mak'st me sit still and sing when I should plough.
When I but think how many a tedious year
150   Our patient Sovereign did attend
        His long misfortune's fatal end;
How cheerfully and how exempt from fear
On the great Sovereign's will he did depend;
I ought to be accurst, if I refuse
To wait on his, O thou fallacious Muse!
Kings have long hands, they say, and though I be
So distant, they may reach at length to me.
        However, of all princes, thou
Shouldst not reproach rewards for being small or slow;
160   Thou who rewardest but with popular breath,
        And that too after death.'

Ode: Upon Dr Harvey

Coy Nature (which remained, though aged grown,
A beauteous virgin still, enjoyed by none,
    Nor seen unveiled by anyone),
When Harvey's violent passion she did see,
Began to tremble and to flee;
Took sanctuary like Daphne in a tree.
There Daphne's lover stopped, and thought it much
    The very leaves of her to touch;
But Harvey, our Apollo, stopped not so;
10   Into the bark and root he after her did go;
        No smallest fibres of a plant,
For which the eye-beams point doth sharpness want,
        His passage after her withstood.
What should she do? Through all the moving wood

Of lives endowed with sense she took her flight;
Harvey pursues and keeps her still in sight.
But as the deer, long hunted, takes a flood,
She leaped at last into the winding streams of blood;
Of man's Meander all the purple reaches made,
20   Till at the heart she stayed;
      Where, turning head and at a bay,
Thus by well-purgèd ears was she o'erheard to say:

'Here sure shall I be safe,' said she;
'None will be able sure to see
      This my retreat but only He
      Who made both it and me.
The heart of man what art can e'er reveal?
      A wall impervious between
      Divides the very parts within,
30 And doth the heart of man ev'n from itself conceal.'
      She spoke, but ere she was aware
      Harvey was with her there,
And held this slippery Proteus in a chain
Till all her mighty mysteries she descried,
Which from his wit the attempt before to hide
Was the first thing that Nature did in vain.

He the young practice of new life did see,
      Whilst to conceal its toilsome poverty
It for a living wrought, both hard and privately;
40   Before the liver understood
      The noble scarlet dye of blood;
      Before one drop was by it made,
Or brought into it, to set up the trade;
Before the untaught heart began to beat
The tuneful march to vital heat,
From all the souls that living buildings rear,
Whether implied for earth or sea or air,
Whether it in the womb or egg be wrought,
A strict account to him is hourly brought

50   How the great fabric does proceed,
What time and what materials it does need.
He so exactly does the work survey
As if he hired the workers by the day.

Thus Harvey sought for Truth in Truth's own book,
    The creatures, which by God himself was writ;
        And wisely thought 'twas fit
Not to read comments only upon it,
But on th' original itself to look.
Methinks in Art's great circle others stand
60   Locked up together, hand in hand;
    Everyone leads as he is led;
    The same bare path they tread,
And dance like fairies a fantastic round,
But neither change their motion nor their ground.
Had Harvey to this road confined his wit,
His noble circle of the blood had been untrodden yet.
Great Doctor! Th' art of curing's cured by thee;
    We now thy patient, Physic, see
From all inveterate diseases free,
70   Purged of old errors by thy care,
New-dieted, put forth to clearer air;
    It now will strong and healthful prove;
Itself before lethargic lay and could not move.

These useful secrets to his pen we owe,
And thousands more 'twas ready to bestow,
Of which a barbarous war's unlearned rage
    Has robbed the ruined age;
O cruel loss! As if the Golden Fleece,
    With so much cost and labour bought,
80   And from afar by a great hero brought,
    Had sunk ev'n in the ports of Greece.
O cursèd war! Who can forgive thee this?
    Houses and towns may rise again,
        And ten times easier it is
To rebuild Paul's than any work of his.

That mighty task none but himself can do,
    Nay, scarce himself too now;
For though his wit the force of Age withstand,
His body, alas, and time it must command;
90 And Nature now, so long by him surpassed,
Will sure have her revenge on him at last.

Ode: 'Acme and Septimius'
Out of Catullus

Acmen Septimius suos amores
Tenens in gremio, &c.

Whilst on Septimius' panting breast
(Meaning nothing less than rest)
Acme leaned her loving head,
Thus the pleased Septimius said:

'My dearest Acme, if I be
Once alive, and love not thee
With a passion far above
All that e'er was callèd love,
In a Lybian desert may
10 I become some lion's prey.
Let him, Acme, let him tear
My breast, when Acme is not there.'

The God of Love who stood to hear him
(The God of Love was always near him),
Pleased and tickled with the sound,
Sneezed aloud, and all around
The little Loves that waited by
Bowed and blessed the augury.

Acme, enflamed with what he said,
20   Reared her gently-bending head
And, her purple mouth with joy
Stretching to the delicious boy,
Twice (and twice could scarce suffice)
She kissed his drunken, rolling eyes.

'My little life, my all,' said she,
'So may we ever servants be
To this best god, and ne'er retain
Our hated liberty again;
So may thy passion last for me
30   As I a passion have for thee,
Greater and fiercer much than can
Be conceived by thee, a man.
Into my marrow is it gone,
Fixed and settled in the bone;
It reigns not only in my heart
But runs, like life, through every part.'

She spoke; the God of Love aloud
Sneezed again, and all the crowd
Of little Loves that waited by
40   Bowed and blessed the augury.

This good omen thus from Heaven
Like a happy signal given,
Their loves and lives (all four) embrace
And hand in hand run all the race.
To poor Septimius (who did now
Nothing else but Acme grow),
Acme's bosom was alone
The whole world's imperial throne;
And to faithful Acme's mind,
50   Septimius was all humankind.

If the gods would please to be
But advised for once by me,
I'd advise 'em, when they spy
Any illustrious piety,
To reward her, if 't be she,
To reward him, if 't be he,
With such a husband, such a wife;
With Acme's and Septimius' life.

The Country Mouse
A Paraphrase upon Horace, Book II, Satire 6

At the large foot of a fair hollow tree,
Close to ploughed ground, seated commodiously,
(His ancient and hereditary house),
There dwelt a good, substantial country mouse;
Frugal and grave, and careful of the main,
Yet one who once did nobly entertain
A city mouse, well-coated, sleek, and gay,
A mouse of high degree, which lost his way,
Wantonly walking forth to take the air,
10   And arrived early, and belighted, there
For a day's lodging; the good hearty host
(The ancient plenty of his hall to boast)
Did all the stores produce that might excite,
With various tastes, the courtier's appetite:
Fitches and beans, peason and oats and wheat,
And a large chestnut, the delicious meat
Which Jove himself, were he a mouse, would eat.
And for a *haut-goust*, there was mixed with these
The swerd of bacon and the coat of cheese,
20   The precious relics which, at harvest, he
Had gathered from the reapers' luxury.
'Freely,' said he, 'fall on and never spare;
The bounteous gods will for tomorrow care.'
And thus at ease on beds of straw they lay
And to their Genius sacrificed the day.

Yet the nice guest's Epicurean mind
(Though breeding made him civil seem and kind)
Despised this country feast, and still his thought
Upon the cakes and pies of London wrought.
30   'Your bounty and civility,' said he,
'Which I'm surprised in these rude parts to see,
Shows that the gods have given you a mind
Too noble for the fate which here you find.
Why should a soul so virtuous and so great
Lose itself thus in an obscure retreat?
Let savage beasts lodge in a country den;
You should see towns, and manners know, and men,
And taste the generous luxury of the Court,
Where all the mice of quality resort;
40   Where thousand beauteous she's about you move,
And by high fare are pliant made to love.
We all ere long must render up our breath;
No cave or hole can shelter us from death.
Since life is so uncertain and so short,
Let's spend it all in feasting and in sport.
Come, worthy Sir, come with me, and partake
All the great things that mortals happy make.'
        Alas, what virtue hath sufficient arms
T' oppose bright Honour and soft Pleasure's charms?
50   What wisdom can their magic force repel?
It draws this reverend hermit from his cell.
It was the time when witty poets tell
'That Phoebus into Thetis' bosom fell;
She blushed at first, and then put out the light,
And drew the modest curtains of the night.'
Plainly, the truth to tell, the sun was set
When to the town our wearied travellers get.
To a lord's house, as lordly as can be,
Made for the use of pride and luxury,
60   They come; the gentle courtier at the door
Stops, and will hardly enter in before;
'But 'tis, Sir, your command; and being so,
I'm sworn t'obedience'; and so in they go.

Behind a hanging in a spacious room
(The richest work of Mortlake's noble loom)
They wait awhile, their wearied limbs to rest,
Till silence should invite them to their feast –
'About the hour that Cynthia's silver light
Had touched the pale meridies of the night.'

70   At last, the various supper being done,
It happened that the company was gone
Into a room remote, servants and all,
To please their noble fancies with a ball.
Our host leads forth his stranger and does find
All fitted to the bounties of his mind.
Still on the table half-filled dishes stood,
And with delicious bits the floor was strowed.
The courteous mouse presents him with the best,
And both with fat varieties are blessed;

80   Th' industrious peasant everywhere does range,
And thanks the gods for his life's happy change.
Lo, in the midst of a well-freighted pie,
They both at last glutted and wanton lie.
When see the sad reverse of prosperous fate,
And what fierce storms on mortal glories wait!
With hideous noise, down the rude servants come;
Six dogs before run barking into th' room;
The wretched gluttons fly with wild affright,
And hate the fullness which retards their flight.

90   Our trembling peasant wishes now in vain
That rocks and mountains covered him again.
O how the change of his poor life he cursed!
'This, of all lives,' said he, 'is sure the worst.
Give me again, ye gods, my cave and wood;
With peace, let tares and acorns be my food.'

The Country Life
from *Libri Plantarum*, Book IV

Blest be the man (and blest he is) whome'er
(Placed far out of the roads of hope or fear)
A little field and little garden feeds:
The field gives all that frugal Nature needs;
The wealthy garden liberally bestows
All she can ask when she luxurious grows.
The specious inconveniences that wait
Upon a life of business and of state
He sees (nor does the sight disturb his rest)
By fools desired, by wicked men possessed.
Thus, thus (and this deserved great Virgil's praise)
The old Corycian yeoman passed his days;
Thus his wise life Abdolominus spent:
Th' ambassadors which the great Emperor sent
To offer him a crown, with wonder found
The reverend gardener hoeing of his ground.
Unwillingly, and slow, and discontent,
From his loved cottage to a throne he went;
And oft he stopped in his triumphant way,
And oft looked back, and oft was heard to say,
Not without sighs, 'Alas, I there forsake
A happier kingdom than I go to take!'
Thus Aglaüs (a man unknown to men,
But the gods knew and therefore loved him then),
Thus lived obscurely then, without a name,
Aglaüs, now consigned t' eternal Fame.
For Gyges, the rich king, wicked and great,
Presumed, at wise Apollo's Delphic seat,
Presumed to ask, 'O thou, the whole world's eye,
See'st thou a man that happier is than I?'
The god, who scorned to flatter man, replied,
'Aglaüs happier is.' But Gyges cried,
In a proud rage, 'Who can that Aglaüs be?
We've heard as yet of no such king as he.'

And true it was through the whole earth around
No king of such a name was to be found.
'Is some old hero of that name alive,
Who his high race does from the gods derive?
Is it some mighty general, that has done
40 Wonders in fight and godlike honours won?
Is it some man of endless wealth?' said he;
'None, none of these; who can this Aglaüs be?'
After long search and vain enquiries passed,
In an obscure Arcadian vale at last
(Th' Arcadian life has always shady been),
Near Sopho's town, which he but once had seen,
This Aglaüs, who monarchs' envy drew,
Whose happiness the gods stood witness to,
This mighty Aglaüs was labouring found
50 With his own hands in his own little ground.

    So, gracious God (if it may lawful be
Among those foolish gods to mention Thee),
So let me act, on such a private stage,
The last dull scenes of my declining age;
After long toils and voyages in vain,
This quiet port let my tossed vessel gain;
Of heav'nly rest this earnest to me lend,
Let my life sleep and learn to love her end.

LIBRI PLANTARUM

from *Book IV*

Felix, quem misera procul ambitione remotum,
    Parvus ager placide, parvus et hortus alit.
Praebet ager quicquid frugi Natura requirit,
    Hortus habet quicquid luxuriosa petit;
Caetera sollicitae speciosa incommoda vitae
    Permittit stultis quaerere, habere malis.

Talis erat magni memoratu digna Maronis
    Corycii quondam vita beata Senis.
Talis (crediderim) tam laetus et impiger hortis
10   Dives in exiguis Abdolominus erat.
Illum damnosas runcantem gnaviter herbas
    Ecce ab Alexandro Rege satelles adit:
'Accipe Sidonii, vir magne, insignia regni,
    Sceptrum,' ait, 'et mitram, Sidoniamque togam.'
Missus in imperium tantum (quis credat?) amatam
    Dicitur invitus deseruisse casam.
Respicit ille gemens hortum; 'Meliōra relinquo,
    Heu,' ait, 'infoelix; deteriora sequor.'
Talis erat generi humano vix nomine notus
20   Aglaus, in parvo Diis bene notus agro.
Namque Gyges Lydas, regum ditissimus olim,
    Impius et scelerum prosperitate tumens,
'Ecquis,' ait, 'toto me fortunatior orbe est?'
    Hic Clarium est ausus voce rogare Deum.
Numen adulari nescit; 'Felicior,' inquit,
    'Aglaus.' Ille furens, 'Aglaus iste quis est?'
An sit eo quisquam rex nomine quaerit; at illo
    Rex certe dictus nomine nullus erat.
An sit eo quisquam dux belli nomine clarus,
30   Aut superis tracta nobilitate potens?
Anne aliquis praedives opum nulloque periclo
    Inter inexhaustas luxuriosus opes?

Nullus erat talis generis splendore, vel armis,
    Divitiisve potens; 'Aglaus iste quis est?'
At tandem Arcadiae vix nota in valle repertus
    (Arcadas alta quies umbraque densa tegit),
Strenuus exigui cultor prope Psophida fundi
    (Psophida sed tantum viderat ille semel)
Invidia regum dignissimus ille repertus,
40   Teste Deo felix, Aglaus ille fuit.
Talis, magne Deus (si te mihi dicere fas sit
    Ridiculorum inter nomina vana Deum)
Talis, vere Deus, nunc inclinantibus annis
    Sit, precor, aetatis scena suprema meae;
Finis inutilium mihi sit precor illa laborum,
    Iactatae statio firma sit illa rati.
Sic mea coelestem praegustet vita quietem;
    Dormiat, et mortem discat amare suam.

Upon the Chair made out of Sir Francis Drake's Ship
Presented to the University Library in Oxford
by John Davis of Deptford, Esquire

To this great ship, which round the globe has run,
And matched in race the chariot of the sun:
This Pythagorean ship (for it may claim
Without presumption so deserved a name,
By knowledge once and transformation now),
In her new shape, this sacred port allow.
Drake and his ship could not have wished from Fate
A more blest station or more blest estate;
For lo, a seat of endless rest is given:
10   To her in Oxford and to him in Heaven.

EDMUND WALLER

Of His Majesty's Receiving the News of the Duke of Buckingham's Death

So earnest with thy God! Can no new care,
No sense of danger, interrupt thy prayer?
The sacred wrestler, till a blessing given,
Quits not his hold but, halting, conquers Heaven;
Nor was the stream of thy devotion stopped
When from the body such a limb was lopped
As to thy present state was no less maim,
Though thy wise choice has since repaired the same.
Bold Homer durst not so great virtue feign
In his best pattern, for Patroclus slain;
With such amazement as weak mothers use,
And frantic gesture, he receives the news.
Yet fell his darling by th' impartial chance
Of war, imposed by royal Hector's lance;
Thine, in full peace and by a vulgar hand
Torn from thy bosom, left his high command.
   The famous painter could allow no place
For private sorrow in a prince's face;
Yet, that his piece might not exceed belief,
He cast a veil upon supposèd grief.
'Twas want of such a precedent as this
Made the old heathen frame their gods amiss;
Their Phoebus should not act a fonder part
For the fair boy than he did for his heart,
Nor blame for Hyacinthus' fate his own,
That kept from him wished death, hadst thou been known.
   He that with thine shall weigh good David's deeds
Shall find his passion, not his love, exceeds.
He cursed the mountains where his brave friend died,
But let false Ziba with his heir divide;
Where thy immortal love to thy best friends,
Like that of Heav'n, upon their seed descends.
Such huge extremes inhabit thy great mind:
God-like, unmoved, and yet, like woman, kind.

10

20

30

Which of the ancient poets had not brought
Our Charles's pedigree from Heav'n, and taught
How some bright dame compressed by mighty Jove
Produced this mixed divinity and love?

To Van Dyck

Rare artisan, whose pencil moves
Not our delights alone, but loves!
From thy shop of beauty, we
Slaves return that entered free.
The heedless lover does not know
Whose eyes they are that wound him so,
But, confounded with thy art,
Inquires her name that has his heart.
Another, who did long refrain,
Feels his old wound bleed fresh again
With dear remembrance of that face
Where now he reads new hopes of grace,
Nor scorn nor cruelty does find,
But gladly suffers a false wind
To blow the ashes of despair
From the reviving brand of care.
Fool, that forgets her stubborn look
This softness from thy finger took!
Strange that thy hand should not inspire
The beauty only but the fire;
Not the form alone and grace,
But act and power of a face.
Mayst thou yet thyself, as well
As all the world besides, excel,
So you th' unfeignèd truth rehearse
(That I may make it live in verse),
Why thou couldst not at one assay
That face to after-times convey
Which this admires. Was it thy wit
To make her oft before thee sit?

Confess and we'll forgive thee this;
For who would not repeat that bliss,
And frequent sight of such a dame
Buy with the hazard of his fame?
Yet who can tax thy blameless skill
Though thy good hand had failèd still,
When Nature's self so often errs?
She for this many thousand years
Seems to have practised with much care
40 To frame the race of women fair,
Yet never could a perfect birth
Produce before to grace the earth,
Which waxèd old, ere it could see
Her that amazed thy art and thee.
   But now 'tis done: O let me know
Where those immortal colours grow
That could this deathless piece compose:
In lilies, or the fading rose?
No, for this theft thou hast climbed higher
50 Than did Prometheus for his fire.

The Story of Phoebus and Daphne Applied

Thyrsis, a youth of the inspirèd train,
Fair Sacharissa loved, but loved in vain:
Like Phoebus sung the no less amorous boy;
Like Daphne she, as lovely and as coy.
With numbers he the flying nymph pursues:
With numbers such as Phoebus' self might use.
Such is the chase, when Love and Fancy leads,
O'er craggy mountains and through flowery meads,
Invoked to testify the lover's care,
10 Or form some image of his cruel fair.
Urged with his fury like a wounded deer,
O'er these he fled, and now approaching near
Had reached the nymph with his harmonious lay,
Whom all his charms could not incline to stay.

Yet what he sang in his immortal strain,
Though unsuccessful, was not sung in vain:
All, but the nymph that should redress his wrong,
Attend his passion and approve his song.
    Like Phoebus thus, acquiring unsought praise,
20   He catched at love and filled his arm with bays.

The Self-Banished

It is not that I love you less
Than when before your feet I lay,
But to prevent the sad increase
Of hopeless love I keep away.

In vain, alas, for everything
Which I have known belong to you,
Your form does to my fancy bring,
And makes my old wounds bleed anew.

Who, in the spring, from the new sun
10   Already has a fever got,
Too late begins those shafts to shun
Which Phoebus through his veins has shot;

Too late he would the pain assuage,
And to thick shadows does retire;
About with him he bears the rage,
And in his tainted blood the fire.

But vowed I have, and never must
Your banished servant trouble you;
For if I break, you may mistrust
20   The vow I made to love you, too.

Song

Go, lovely rose:
Tell her, that wastes her time and me,
　That now she knows,
When I resemble her to thee,
　How sweet and fair she seems to be.

Tell her, that's young,
And shuns to have her graces spied,
　That hadst thou sprung
In deserts, where no men abide,
Thou must have uncommended died.

Small is the worth
Of beauty, from the light retired;
　Bid her come forth,
Suffer herself to be desired,
　And not blush so to be admired.

Then die, that she
The common fate of all things rare
　May read in thee;
How small a part of time they share,
　That are so wondrous sweet and fair.

from *The Battle of the Summer Islands*

CANTO I

What fruits they have, and how Heav'n smiles
Upon those late-discovered isles.

Aid me, Bellona, while the dreadful fight
Betwixt a nation and two whales I write.
Seas stained with gore I sing, adventurous toil,

And how these monsters did disarm an isle.
    Bermudas, walled with rocks, who does not know?
That happy island, where huge lemons grow,
And orange trees which golden fruit do bear –
Th' Hesperian Garden boasts of none so fair;
Where shining pearl, coral, and many a pound,
On the rich shore, of ambergris is found.
The lofty cedar, which to Heav'n aspires
(The prince of trees), is fuel for their fires;
The smoke by which their loaded spits do turn,
For incense might on sacred altars burn;
Their private roofs, on odorous timber borne,
Such as might palaces for kings adorn.
The sweet palmettos a new Bacchus yield,
With leaves as ample as the broadest shield,
Under the shadow of whose friendly boughs
They sit carousing where their liquor grows.
Figs there, unplanted, through the fields do grow,
Such as fierce Cato did the Romans show,
With the rare fruit inviting them to spoil
Carthage, the mistress of so rich a soil.
The naked rocks are not unfruitful there,
But, at some constant seasons every year,
Their barren tops with luscious food abound,
And with the eggs of various fowls are crowned.
Tobacco is the worst of things, which they
To English landlords as their tribute pay;
Such is the mould, that the blest tenant feeds
On precious fruits and pays his rent in weeds.
With candied plantains and the juicy pine,
On choicest melons and sweet grapes they dine,
And with potatoes fat their wanton swine.
Nature these cates with such a lavish hand
Pours out among them, that our coarser land
Tastes of that bounty and does cloth return,
Which not for warmth but ornament is worn;
For the kind Spring, which but salutes us here,
Inhabits there and courts them all the year.

Ripe fruits and blossoms on the same trees live:
At once they promise what at once they give.
So sweet the air, so moderate the clime,
None sickly lives, or dies before his time.
Heav'n sure has kept this spot of earth uncursed,
To show how all things were created first.
The tardy plants in our cold orchards placed
Reserve their fruit for the next age's taste;
50   There, a small grain in some few months will be
A firm, a lofty, and a spacious tree:
The palma-christi and the fair papaw
(Now but a seed), preventing Nature's law,
In half the circle of the hasty year
Project a shade and lovely fruit do wear.
And as their trees, in our dull region set,
But faintly grow and no perfection get,
So, in this northern tract, our hoarser throats
Utter unripe and ill-constrainèd notes,
60   Where the supporter of the poet's style,
Phoebus, on them eternally does smile.
O how I long my careless limbs to lay
Under the plantain's shade, and all the day
With amorous airs my fancy entertain,
Invoke the Muses, and improve my vein!
No passion there in my free breast should move –
None but the sweet and best of passions, Love:
There while I sing, if gentle Love be by,
That tunes my lute and winds the strings so high,
70   With the sweet sound of Sacharissa's name
I'll make the listening savages grow tame.

To Phyllis

Phyllis, why should we delay
Pleasures shorter than the day?
Could we (which we never can)
Stretch our lives beyond their span,

Beauty like a shadow flies,
And our youth before us dies;
Or would youth and beauty stay,
Love hath wings and will away.
Love hath swifter wings than Time;
10 Change in love to Heav'n does climb.
Gods, that never change their state,
Vary oft their love and hate.
Phyllis, to this truth we owe
All the love betwixt us two.
Let not you and I require
What has been our past desire;
On what shepherds you have smiled,
Or what nymphs I have beguiled;
Leave it to the planets, too,
20 What we shall hereafter do;
For the joys we now may prove,
Take advice of present love.

To my Lord of Falkland

Brave Holland leads and with him Falkland goes.
Who hears this told and does not straight suppose
We send the Graces and the Muses forth,
To civilize and to instruct the north?
   Not that these ornaments make swords less sharp:
Apollo bears as well his bow as harp,
And though he be the patron of that spring
Where, in calm peace, the sacred virgins sing,
He courage had to guard th' invaded throne
10 Of Jove, and cast th' ambitious Giants down.
   Ah, noble Friend, with what impatience all
That know thy worth, and know how prodigal
Of thy great soul thou art, longing to twist
Bays with that ivy which so early kissed
Thy youthful temples – with what horror we
Think on the blind events of war, and thee?

To Fate exposing that all-knowing breast
Among the throng, as cheaply as the rest;
Where oaks and brambles (if the copse be burned)
20   Confounded lie, to the same ashes turned.
      Some happy wind over the ocean blow
This tempest yet, which frights our island so;
Guarded with ships, and all the sea our own,
From Heav'n this mischief on our heads is thrown.
      In a late dream, the Genius of this land,
Amazed, I saw like the fair Hebrew stand,
When first she felt the twins begin to jar,
And found her womb the seat of civil war.
Inclined to whose relief, and with presage
30   Of better fortune for the present age,
'Heav'n sends,' quoth I, 'this discord for our good,
To warm, perhaps, but not to waste our blood;
To raise our drooping spirits, grown the scorn
Of our proud neighbours, who ere long shall mourn
(Though now they joy in our expected harms)
We had occasion to resume our arms.'
      A lion so, with self-provoking smart,
His rebel tail scourging his nobler part,
Calls up his courage; then begins to roar,
40   And charge his foes, who thought him mad before.

For Drinking of Healths

Let brutes and vegetals, that cannot think,
So far as drought and Nature urges, drink;
A more indulgent mistress guides our sprites,
Reason, that dares beyond our appetites.
She would our care as well as thirst redress,
And with divinity rewards excess.
Deserted Ariadne, thus supplied,
Did perjured Theseus' cruelty deride;
Bacchus embraced, from her exalted thought
10   Banished the man, her passion, and his fault.

Bacchus and Phoebus are by Jove allied,
And each by other's timely heat supplied;
All that the grapes owe to his ripening fires
Is paid in numbers which their juice inspires.
Wine fills the veins, and healths are understood
To give our friends a title to our blood;
Who, naming me, doth warm his courage so
Shows for my sake what his bold hand would do.

Of the Marriage of the Dwarfs

Design or Chance makes others wive,
But Nature did this match contrive;
Eve might as well have Adam fled
As she denied her little bed
To him, for whom Heav'n seemed to frame
And measure out this only dame.

Thrice happy is that humble pair,
Beneath the level of all care,
Over whose heads those arrows fly
10 Of sad Distrust and Jealousy,
Securèd in as high extreme
As if the world held none but them.

To him the fairest nymphs do show
Like moving mountains topped with snow,
And every man a Polypheme
Does to his Galatea seem;
None may presume her faith to prove:
He proffers death that proffers love.

Ah, Chloris, that kind Nature thus
20 From all the world had severed us,
Creating for ourselves us two,
As Love has me for only you!

From a Child

Madam,
As in some climes the warmer sun
Makes it full summer ere the spring's begun,
And with ripe fruit the bending boughs can load
Before our violets dare look abroad:
So measure not by any common use
The early love your brighter eyes produce.
When lately your fair hand in women's weed
Wrapped my glad head, I wished me so indeed,
That hasty Time might never make me grow
Out of those favours you afford me now;
That I might ever such indulgence find,
And you not blush or think yourself too kind,
Who now, I fear, while I these joys express,
Begin to think how you may make them less;
The sound of love makes your soft heart afraid
And guard itself, though but a child invade,
And innocently at your white breast throw
A dart as white, a ball of new-fall'n snow.

On a Girdle

That which her slender waist confined
Shall now my joyful temples bind;
No monarch but would give his crown
His arms might do what this has done.

It was my Heav'n's extremest sphere,
The pale which held that lovely dear;
My joy, my grief, my hope, my love
Did all within this circle move.

A narrow compass, and yet there
10   Dwelt all that's good and all that's fair;
Give me but what this ribbon bound,
Take all the rest the sun goes round.

The Apology of Sleep

For not approaching the lady who can do anything but sleep when
she pleaseth.

My charge it is those breaches to repair
Which Nature takes from sorrow, toil, and care.
Rest to the limbs, and quiet I confer
On troubled minds; but nought can add to her,
Whom Heav'n and her transcendent thoughts have placed
Above those ills which wretched mortals taste.
   Bright as the deathless gods and happy, she
From all that may infringe delight is free;
Love at her royal feet his quiver lays,
10   And not his mother with more haste obeys.
Such real pleasures', such true joys' suspense,
What dream can I present to recompense?
Should I with lightning fill her awful hand,
And make the clouds seem all at her command,
Or place her in Olympus' top, a guest
Among th' immortals who with nectar feast:
That power would seem, that entertainment, short
Of the true splendour of her present Court,
Where all the joys and all the glories are
20   Of three great kingdoms, severed from the care.
I that, of fumes and humid vapours made,
Ascending, do the seat of sense invade,
No cloud in so serene a mansion find
To overcast her ever-shining mind,
Which holds resemblance with those spotless skies
Where flowing Nilus want of rain supplies;

That crystal heav'n, where Phoebus never shrouds
His golden beams, nor wraps his face in clouds.
    But what so hard which numbers cannot force?
30 So stoops the moon and rivers change their course;
The bold Maeonian made me dare to steep
Jove's dreadful temples in the dew of sleep.
And since the Muses do invoke my power,
I shall no more decline that sacred bower
Where Gloriana their great mistress lies,
But, gently taming those victorious eyes,
Charm all her senses, till the joyful sun
Without a rival half his course has run;
Who, while my hand that fairer light confines,
40 May boast himself the brightest thing that shines.

[At Penshurst]

Had Sacharissa lived when mortals made
Choice of their deities, this sacred shade
Had held an altar to her power, that gave
The peace and glory which these alleys have;
Embroidered so with flowers where she stood
That it became a garden of a wood.
Her presence has such more than human grace
That it can civilize the rudest place,
And beauty too and order can impart
10 Where Nature ne'er intended it, nor Art.
The plants acknowledge this, and her admire
No less than those of old did Orpheus' lyre:
If she sit down, with tops all towards her bowed
They round about her into arbours crowd;
Or, if she walk, in even ranks they stand,
Like some well-marshalled and obsequious band.
Amphion so made stones and timber leap
Into fair figures from a confused heap,
And in the symmitry of her parts is found
20 A power like that of harmony in sound.

Ye lofty beeches, tell this matchless dame
That if together ye fed all one flame,
It could not equalize the hundredth part
Of what her eyes have kindled in my heart.
Go, boy, and carve this passion on the bark
Of yonder tree, which stands the sacred mark
Of noble Sidney's birth, when such benign,
Such more-than-mortal-making stars did shine,
That there they cannot but for ever prove
30   The monument and pledge of humble love:
His humble love, whose hope shall ne'er rise higher
Than for a pardon that he dares admire.

Song

Behold the brand of Beauty tossed:
See how the motion does dilate the flame;
Delighted Love his spoils does boast,
   And triumph in this game.
Fire, to no place confined,
Is both our wonder and our fear,
   Moving the mind
As lightning hurlèd through the air.

High Heav'n the glory does increase
10   Of all her shining lamps this artful way;
The sun in figures such as these
   Joys with the moon to play.
To the sweet strains they advance
Which do result from their own spheres;
   As this nymph's dance
Moves with the numbers which she hears.

A la Malade

Ah lovely Amoret, the care
Of all that know what's good or fair,
Is Heav'n become our rival too?
Had the rich gifts, conferred on you
So amply thence, the common end
Of giving lovers – to pretend?
   Hence to this pining sickness (meant
To weary thee to a consent
Of leaving us) no power is given
Thy beauties to impair; for Heaven
Solicits thee with such a care
As roses from their stalks we tear
When we would still preserve them new
And fresh as on the bush they grew.
   With such a grace you entertain,
And look with such contempt on pain,
That, languishing, you conquer more
And wound us deeper than before.
So lightnings, which in storms appear,
Scorch more than when the skies are clear.
And as pale sickness does invade
Your frailer part, the breaches made
In that fair lodging still more clear
Make the bright guest, your soul, appear.
So nymphs, o'er pathless mountains borne,
Their light robes by the brambles torn
From their fair limbs, exposing new
And unknown beauties to the view
Of following gods, increase their flame
And haste to catch the flying game.

To the Mutable Fair

Here, Celia, for thy sake I part
With all that grew so near my heart:
The passion that I had for thee,
The faith, the love, the constancy;
And that I may successful prove,
Transform myself to what you love.

    Fool that I was, so much to prize
Those simple virtues you despise –
Fool, that with such dull arrows strove,
Or hoped to reach a flying dove!
For you, that are in motion still,
Decline our force and mock our skill,
Who like Don Quixote do advance
Against a windmill our vain lance.

    Now will I wander through the air,
Mount, make a stoop at every fair,
And with a fancy unconfined
(As lawless as the sea or wind)
Pursue you wheresoe'er you fly,
And with your various thoughts comply.

    The formal stars do travel so
As we their names and courses know;
And he that on their changes looks
Would think them governed by our books.
But never were the clouds reduced
To any art: the motions used
By those free vapours are so light,
So frequent, that the conquered sight
Despairs to find the rules that guide
Those gilded shadows as they slide.
And therefore of the spacious air
Jove's royal consort had the care,
And by that power did once escape,
Declining bold Ixion's rape;
She with her own resemblance graced
A shining cloud, which he embraced.

Such was that image, so it smiled,
With seeming kindness which beguiled
Your Thyrsis lately, when he thought
He had his fleeting Celia caught.
'Twas shaped like her; but for the fair
He filled his arms with yielding air.
A fate for which he grieves the less,
Because the gods had like success.
For in their story, one, we see,
Pursues a nymph and takes a tree;
A second, with a lover's haste,
Soon overtakes whom he had chased;
But she that did a virgin seem,
Possessed, appears a wandering stream.
For his supposèd love, a third
Lays greedy hold upon a bird,
And stands amazed to find his dear
A wild inhabitant of th' air.
To these old tales, such nymphs as you
Give credit, and still make them new;
The amorous now like wonders find
In the swift changes of your mind.
But, Celia, if you apprehend
The Muse of your incensèd friend,
Nor would that he record your blame
And make it live, repeat the same;
Again deceive him, and again,
And then he swears he'll not complain.
For still to be deluded so
Is all the pleasure lovers know,
Who, like good falconers, take delight
Not in the quarry but the flight.

In Answer of Sir John Suckling's Verses

Con.
Stay here, fond youth, and ask no more, be wise;
Knowing too much long since lost Paradise.

Pro.
And by your knowledge, we should be bereft
Of all that Paradise which yet is left.

Con.
The virtuous joys thou hast, thou wouldst should still
Last in their pride; and wouldst not take it ill
If rudely from sweet dreams, and for a toy,
Thou waked? He wakes himself that does enjoy.

Pro.
How can the joy or hope which you allow
10   Be stylèd virtuous, and the end not so?
Talk in your sleep and shadows still admire;
'Tis true he wakes that feels this real fire,
But to sleep better; for whoe'er drinks deep
Of this nepenthe, rocks himself asleep.

Con.
Fruition adds no new wealth but destroys,
And while it pleaseth much, yet still it cloys:
Who thinks he should be happier made for that,
As reasonably might hope he might grow fat
By eating to a surfeit; this once past,
20   What relishes? Ev'n kisses lose their taste.

Pro.
Blessings may be repeated while they cloy;
But shall we starve 'cause surfeitings destroy?
And if fruition did the taste impair

Of kisses, why should yonder happy pair,
Whose joys just Hymen warrants all the night,
Consume the day too in this less delight?

Con.
Urge not 'tis necessary; alas, we know
The homeliest thing that mankind does, is so.
The world is of a large extent, we see,
30   And must be peopled; children there must be.
So must bread too; but since there are enough
Born to that drudgery, what need we plough?

Pro.
I need not plough, since what the stooping hind
Gets of my pregnant land must all be mine;
But in this nobler tillage 'tis not so;
For when Anchises did fair Venus know,
What interest had poor Vulcan in the boy
(Famous Aeneas), or the present joy?

Con.
Women enjoyed, whate'ertofore they've been,
40   Are like romances read or scenes once seen;
Fruition dulls or spoils the play much more
Than if one read or know the plot before.

Pro.
Plays and romances read and seen do fall
In our opinions, yet not seen at all
Whom would they please? To an heroic tale
Would you not listen lest it should grow stale?

Con.
'Tis expectation makes a blessing dear;
Heav'n were not Heav'n if we knew what it were.

Pro.
If 'twere not Heav'n if we knew what it were,
50   'Twould not be Heav'n to those that now are there.

Con.

As in prospects we are there pleasèd most
Where something keeps the eye from being lost
And leaves us room to guess; so here, restraint
Holds up delight that with excess would faint.

Pro.

Restraint preserves the pleasure we have got,
But he ne'er has it that enjoys it not.
In goodly prospects who contracts the space,
Or takes not all the bounty of the place?
We wish removed what standeth in our light
60 And Nature blame for limiting our sight,
Where you stand wisely winking, that the view
Of the fair prospect may be always new.

Con.

They who know all the wealth they have are poor;
He's only rich that cannot tell his store.

Pro.

Not he that knows the wealth he has is poor,
But he that dares not touch nor use his store.

On Mr John Fletcher's Plays

Fletcher, to thee we do not only owe
All these good plays, but those of others too.
Thy wit, repeated, does support the stage,
Credits the last and entertains this age;
No worthies formed by any Muse but thine
Could purchase robes to make themselves so fine.
　　What brave commander is not proud to see
Thy brave Melantius in his gallantry?
Our greatest ladies love to see their scorn
10 Out-done by thine in what themselves have worn;

Th' impatient widow, ere the year be done,
Sees thy Aspasia weeping in her gown.
    I never yet the tragic strain assayed,
Deterred by that inimitable Maid;
And when I venture at the comic style,
Thy Scornful Lady seems to mock my toil.
    Thus has thy Muse at once improved and marred
Our sport in plays, by rendering it too hard;
So when a sort of lusty shepherds throw
20 The bar by turns, and none the rest outgo
So far, but that the best are measuring casts,
Their emulation and their pastime lasts;
But if some brawny yeoman of the guard
Step in, and toss the axletree a yard
Or more beyond the furthest mark – the rest
Despairing stand; their sport is at the best.

A Panegyric to my Lord Protector

While, with a strong and yet a gentle hand,
You bridle faction and our hearts command,
Protect us from ourselves and from the foe,
Make us unite, and make us conquer too:
Let partial spirits still aloud complain,
Think themselves injured that they cannot reign,
And own no liberty, but where they may
Without control upon their fellows prey.
    Above the waves as Neptune showed his face
10 To chide the winds and save the Trojan race,
So has your Highness, raised above the rest,
Storms of ambition, tossing us, repressed.
Your drooping country, torn with civil hate,
Restored by you is made a glorious state;
The seat of empire, where the Irish come
And the unwilling Scotch, to fetch their doom.
The sea's our own, and now all nations greet
With bending sails each vessel of our fleet;

Your power extends as far as winds can blow,
Or swelling sails upon the globe may go.
    Heav'n, that has placed this island to give law,
To balance Europe, and her states to awe,
In this conjunction does on Britain smile:
The greatest leader and the greatest isle.
Whether this portion of the world were rent
By the rude ocean from the Continent,
Or thus created, it was sure designed
To be the sacred refuge of mankind.
Hither th' oppressèd shall henceforth resort,
Justice to crave, and succour, at your Court;
And then your Highness, not for ours alone,
But for the world's Protector shall be known.
Fame, swifter than your wingèd navy, flies
Through every land that near the ocean lies,
Sounding your name, and telling dreadful news
To all that piracy and rapine use.
With such a chief the meanest nation blessed
Might hope to lift her head above the rest;
What may be thought impossible to do
For us, embracèd by the sea and you?
    Lords of the world's great waste, the Ocean, we
Whole forests send to reign upon the sea,
And ev'ry coast may trouble or relieve;
But none can visit us without your leave.
Angels and we have this prerogative,
That none can at our happy seat arrive,
While we descend at pleasure, to invade
The bad with vengeance, or the good to aid.
Our little world, the image of the great,
Like that, amidst the boundless ocean set,
Of her own growth has all that Nature craves,
And all that's rare, as tribute from the waves;
As Egypt does not on the clouds rely,
But to her Nile owes more than to the sky,
So what our earth and what our heav'n denies,
Our ever-constant friend, the sea, supplies;

The taste of hot Arabia's spice we know,
Free from the scorching sun that makes it grow;
Without the worm, in Persian silks we shine,
60   And without planting drink of every vine.
    To dig for wealth we weary not our limbs:
Gold, though the heaviest metal, hither swims;
Ours is the harvest where the Indians mow;
We plough the deep and reap what others sow.
Things of the noblest kind our own soil breeds:
Stout are our men and warlike are our steeds;
Rome, though her eagle through the world had flown,
Could never make this island all her own.
Here the third Edward, and the Black Prince too,
70   France-conquering Henry flourished, and now you –
For whom we stayed, as did the Grecian state
Till Alexander came to urge their fate.
    When for more worlds the Macedonian cried,
He wist not Thetis in her lap did hide
Another yet, a world reserved for you
To make more great than that he did subdue;
He safely might old troops to battle lead
Against th'unwarlike Persian and the Mede,
Whose hasty flight did, from a bloodless field,
80   More spoil than honour to the victor yield.
    A race unconquered, by their clime made bold,
The Caledonians, armed with want and cold,
Have, by a fate indulgent to your fame,
Been, from all ages, kept for you to tame;
Whom the old Roman wall so ill confined,
With a new chain of garrisons you bind;
Here foreign gold no more shall make them come:
Our English iron holds them fast at home.
They, that henceforth must be content to know
90   No warmer region then their hills of snow,
May blame the sun, but must extol your grace,
Which in our senate has allowed them place;
Preferred by conquest, happily o'erthrown,
Falling they rise, to be with us made one;

So kind dictators made, when they came home,
Their vanquished foes free citizens of Rome.
    Like favour find the Irish, with like fate
Advanced to be a portion of our State;
While, by your valour and your courteous mind,
100   Nations, divided by the sea, are joined.
    Holland, to gain your friendship, is content
To be our out-guard on the Continent;
She from her fellow-provinces would go,
Rather than hazard to have you her foe.
In our late fight, when cannons did diffuse
(Preventing posts) the terror and the news,
Our neighbour-princes trembled at their roar;
But our conjunction makes them tremble more.
    Your never-failing sword made war to cease,
110   And now you heal us with the arts of peace;
Our minds with bounty and with awe engage,
Invite affections and restrain our rage.
Less pleasure take brave minds in battles won
Then in restoring such as are undone;
Tigers have courage and the rugged bear,
But man alone can, whom he conquers, spare.
To pardon willing and to punish loath,
You strike with one hand but you heal with both;
Lifting up all that prostrate lie, you grieve
120   You cannot make the dead again to live.
    When Fate or Error had our age misled,
And o'er these nations such confusion spread,
The only cure which could from Heav'n come down
Was so much power and clemency in one –
One, whose extraction from an ancient line
Gives hope again that well-born men may shine;
The meanest, in your nature, mild and good,
The noble rest securèd in your blood.
    Oft have we wondered how you hid in peace
130   A mind proportioned to such things as these;
How such a ruling spirit you could restrain,
And practise first over yourself to reign.
Your private life did a just pattern give

How fathers, husbands, pious sons should live;
Born to command, your princely virtues slept
Like humble David's while the flock he kept;
But when your troubled country called you forth,
Your flaming courage and your matchless worth,
Dazzling the eyes of all that did pretend,
140   To fierce contention gave a prosperous end.
Still as you rise, the State, exalted too,
Finds no distemper while 'tis changed by you;
Changed like the world's great scene, when without noise
The rising sun night's vulgar lights destroys.

    Had you some ages past this race of glory
Run, with amazement we should read your story;
But living Virtue, all achievements past,
Meets Envy still to grapple with at last.
This Caesar found, and that ungrateful age
150   Which, losing him, fell back to blood and rage;
Mistaken Brutus thought to break their yoke,
But cut the bond of union with that stroke.
That sun once set, a thousand meaner stars
Gave a dim light to violence and wars;
To such a tempest as now threatens all,
Did not your mighty arm prevent the fall.

    If Rome's great senate could not wield that sword
Which of the conquered world had made them lord,
What hope had ours, while yet their power was new,
160   To rule victorious armies, but by you?
You that had taught them to subdue their foes,
Could order teach and their high spirits compose;
To every duty could their minds engage,
Provoke their courage and command their rage.
So, when a lion shakes his dreadful mane
And angry grows, if he that first took pain
To tame his youth approach the haughty beast,
He bends to him but frights away the rest.
As the vexed world, to find repose at last,
170   Itself into Augustus' arms did cast;
So England now does, with like toil oppressed,
Her weary head upon your bosom rest.

Then let the Muses with such notes as these
Instruct us what belongs unto our peace.
Your battles they hereafter shall indite,
And draw the image of our Mars in fight:
Tell of towns stormed, of armies over-run,
And mighty kingdoms by your conduct won;
How while you thundered, clouds of dust did choke
180   Contending troops, and seas lay hid in smoke.
Illustrious acts high raptures do infuse,
And every conqueror creates a Muse.
  Here in low strains your milder deeds we sing,
But there, my Lord, we'll bays and olive bring
To crown your head, while you in triumph ride
O'er vanquished nations and the sea beside;
While all your neighbour-princes unto you,
Like Joseph's sheaves, pay reverence and bow.

Prologue for the Lady Actors

Amaze us not with that majestic frown,
But lay aside the greatness of your crown.
For your diversion here we act in jest;
But when we act ourselves, we do our best.
You have a look which does your people awe,
When in your throne and robes you give 'em law;
Lay it by here and use a gentler smile,
Such as we see great Jove's in picture, while
He listens to Apollo's charming lyre,
10   Or judges of the songs he does inspire.
Comedians on the stage show all their skill,
And after do as Love and Fortune will.
We are less careful, hid in this disguise;
In our own clothes more serious and more wise.
Modest at home, upon the stage more bold,
We seem warm lovers though our breasts be cold.
A fault committed here deserves no scorn,
If we act well the parts to which we're born.

On St James's Park
As lately improved by His Majesty

Of the first Paradise there's nothing found:
Plants set by Heav'n are vanished, and the ground.
Yet the description lasts; who knows the fate
Of lines that shall this paradise relate?
   Instead of rivers, rolling by the side
Of Eden's garden, here flows in the tide;
The sea, which always served his empire, now
Pays tribute to our Prince's pleasure too.
Of famous cities we the founders know;
But rivers, old as seas, to which they go,
Are Nature's bounty; 'tis of more renown
To make a river than to build a town.
For future shade, young trees upon the banks
Of the new stream appear in even ranks;
The voice of Orpheus or Amphion's hand
In better order could not make them stand.
May they increase as fast, and spread their boughs,
As the high fame of their great owner grows!
May he live long enough to see them all
Dark shadows cast, and as his palace tall!
Methinks I see the love that shall be made,
The lovers walking in that amorous shade;
The gallants dancing by the river's side;
They bathe in summer and in winter slide.
Methinks I hear the music in the boats,
And the loud echo which returns the notes,
Whilst overhead a flock of new-sprung fowl
Hangs in the air and does the sun control;
Darkening the sky, they hover o'er and shroud
The wanton sailors with a feathered cloud.
Beneath, a shoal of silver fishes glides,
And plays about the gilded barges' sides;
The ladies, angling in the crystal lake,
Feast on the waters with the prey they take;

At once victorious with their lines and eyes,
They make the fishes and the men their prize.
A thousand cupids on the billows ride,
And sea-nymphs enter with the swelling tide,
From Thetis sent as spies, to make report
40 And tell the wonders of her sovereign's court.
All that can, living, feed the greedy eye,
Or dead, the palate, here you may descry:
The choicest things that furnished Noah's Ark,
Or Peter's sheet, inhabiting this park;
All with a border of rich fruit trees crowned,
Whose loaded branches hide the lofty mound.
Such various ways the spacious alleys lead,
My doubtful Muse knows not what path to tread;
Yonder the harvest of cold months laid up
50 Gives a fresh coolness to the royal cup;
There ice, like crystal, firm and never lost,
Tempers hot July with December's frost –
Winter's dark prison, whence he cannot fly,
Though the warm Spring, his enemy, draws nigh.
Strange that extremes should thus preserve the snow:
High on the Alps or in deep caves below!
    Here a well-polished Mall gives us the joy
To see our Prince his matchless force employ;
His manly posture and his graceful mien,
60 Vigour and youth in all his motion seen,
His shape so lovely and his limbs so strong,
Confirm our hopes we shall obey him long.
No sooner has he touched the flying ball
But 'tis already more than half the Mall,
And such a fury from his arm has got
As from a smoking culverin 'twere shot.
    Near this my Muse what most delights her sees:
A living gallery of agèd trees;
Bold sons of earth, that thrust their arms so high
70 As if once more they would invade the sky.
In such green palaces the first kings reigned,
Slept in their shades, and angels entertained;

With such old counsellors they did advise,
And by frequenting sacred groves grew wise.
Free from th' impediments of light and noise,
Man, thus retired, his nobler thoughts employs;
Here Charles contrives the ordering of his states;
Here he resolves his neighbouring princes' fates;
What nation shall have peace, where war be made,
80   Determined is in this oraculous shade;
The world, from India to the frozen north,
Concerned in what this solitude brings forth.
His fancy, objects from his view receives;
The prospect, thought and contemplation gives.
That seat of empire here salutes his eye,
To which three kingdoms do themselves apply:
The structure by a prelate raised, Whitehall,
Built with the fortune of Rome's Capitol –
Both, disproportioned to the present state
90   Of their proud founders, were approved by Fate.
From hence he does that antique pile behold
Where royal heads receive the sacred gold;
It gives them crowns and does their ashes keep;
There made like gods, like mortals there they sleep,
Making the circle of their reign complete:
Those suns of empire! Where they rise they set.
When others fell, this, standing, did presage
The Crown should triumph over popular rage;
Hard by that House where all our ills were shaped
100   Th' auspicious temple stood, and yet escaped.
So snow on Etna does unmelted lie,
Whence rolling flames and scattered cinders fly;
The distant country in the ruin shares;
What falls from Heav'n the burning mountain spares.
Next, that capacious Hall he sees, the room
Where the whole nation does for justice come,
Under whose large roof flourishes the gown,
And judges grave on high tribunals frown.
Here like the people's Pastor he does go,
110   His flock subjected to his view below;

On which reflecting in his mighty mind,
No private passion does indulgence find;
The pleasures of his youth suspended are,
And made a sacrifice to public care.
Here, free from Court compliances, he walks,
And with himself, his best adviser, talks;
How peaceful olive may his temples shade
For mending laws and for restoring trade;
Or how his brows may be with laurel charged
120 For nations conquered and our bounds enlarged.
Of ancient prudence here he ruminates,
Of rising kingdoms and of falling states;
What ruling arts gave great Augustus fame,
And how Alcides purchased such a name.
His eyes, upon his native palace bent
Close by, suggest a greater argument:
His thoughts rise higher when he does reflect
On what the world may from that star expect
Which at his birth appeared, to let us see
130 Day for his sake could with the night agree;
A Prince on whom such different lights did smile,
Born the divided world to reconcile.
Whatever Heav'n or high extracted blood
Could promise or foretell, he will make good;
Reform these nations, and improve them more
Than this fair park from what it was before.

Instructions to a Painter
*For the Drawing of a Picture of the State and Posture of the
English Forces at Sea, under the Command of his Royal
Highness, in the Conclusion of the year 1664*

First draw the sea, that portion which between
The greater world and this of ours is seen;
Here place the British, there the Holland fleet,
Vast floating armies, both prepared to meet.

Draw the whole world expecting who shall reign,
After this combat, o'er the conquered main;
Make Heav'n concerned, and an unusual star
Declare th' importance of th' approaching war.

Make the sea shine with gallantry, and all
10 The English youth flock to their Admiral,
The valiant Duke, whose early deeds abroad
Such rage in fight and art in conduct showed.
His bright sword, now, a dearer interest draws:
His brother's glory and his country's cause.

Let thy bold pencil hope and courage spread
Through the whole navy by his Highness led;
Make all appear, where such a prince is by,
Resolved to conquer or resolved to die.

With his extraction and heroic mind
20 Make the proud sails swell more than with the wind;
Preventing cannon, make his louder fame
Check the Batavians and their fury tame.
So hungry wolves, though greedy of their prey,
Stop, when they find a lion in their way.

Make him bestride the ocean, and mankind
Ask his consent to use the sea and wind;
While his tall ships in the barred Channel stand,
He grasps the Indies in his armèd hand.

Paint an east wind, and make it blow away
30 Th'excuse of Holland for their navy's stay;
Make them look pale, and, the bold Prince to shun,
Through the cold north and rocky regions run;
To find the coast where morning first appears,
By the dark Pole the wary Belgian steers,
Confessing now he dreads the English more
Than all the dangers of a frozen shore;
While from our arms, security to find,
They fly so far they leave the day behind.

Describe their fleet abandoning the sea,
40   And all their merchants left a wealthy prey.

Our first success in war make Bacchus crown,
And half the vintage of the year our own;
The Dutch their wine and all their brandy lose,
Disarmed of that from which their courage grows,
While the glad English, to relieve their toil,
In healths to their great leader drink the spoil.

His high command to Afric's coast extend,
And make the Moor before the English bend;
Those barbarous pirates willingly receive
50   Conditions such as we are pleased to give.

Within those straights, make Holland's Smyrna fleet
With a small squadron of the English meet;
Like falcons these, those like a numerous flock
Of scattering fowl, which would avoid the shock.

There paint confusion in a various shape:
Some sink, some yield, and, flying, some escape;
Europe and Africa, from either shore,
Spectators are and hear our cannon roar.

While the divided world in this agree:
60   Men that fight so, deserve to rule the sea.

Upon Her Majesty's New Buildings at Somerset House

Great Queen, that does our island bless
With princes and with palaces;
Treated so ill, chased from your throne,
Returning, you adorn the town,
And with a brave revenge do show
Their glory went and came with you.

While peace from hence, and you, were gone,
Your houses in that storm o'erthrown,
Those wounds which civil rage did give
10   At once you pardon and relieve;
    Constant to England in your love
As birds are to their wonted grove:
Though by rude hands their nests are spoiled,
There, the next spring, again they build.

    Accusing some malignant star,
Not Britain, for that fatal war,
Your kindness banishes your fear,
Resolved to fix forever here.

    But what new mine this work supplies?
20   Can such a pile from ruin rise?
This like the first Creation shows,
As if at your command it rose.

    Frugality, and bounty too,
(Those differing virtues) meet in you;
From a confined, well-managed store
You both employ and feed the poor.

    Let foreign princes vainly boast
The rude effects of pride and cost
Of vaster fabrics, to which they
30   Contribute nothing but the pay;
This, by the Queen herself designed,
Gives us a pattern of her mind;
The state and order does proclaim
The genius of that royal dame,
Each part with just proportion graced,
And all to such advantage placed
That the fair view her window yields,
The town, the river, and the fields,
Entering, beneath us we descry,
40   And wonder how we came so high.

    She needs no weary steps ascend;
All seems before her feet to bend,
And here, as she was born, she lies:
High, without taking pains to rise.

[Sir John and Lady Denham]

Methinks her beauty should revive his quill:
The prospect's fairer than his *Cooper's Hill*.
Since he that mountain for Parnassus took,
Why should he not for Helicon this Brooke?
At once the poet for declining age
Has got a staff, and subject for his rage.

Why should men wonder at this marriage thus?
The proverb makes the lame man lecherous;
Wisely the nymph has made her choice of one
Who cannot after other beauties run.
Suppose he had nor foot nor t'other limb:
He that can neither stand nor go may swim.
'Tis said he had the royal leave to woo;
He that asks leave, of right should give it, too.
The loves of brooks no person should restrain:
Through several grounds they roll into the main;
Those streams of crystal, like the light and wind,
Enjoyed may be but should not be confined.

To be the wife of him which downright halts
Both sets off virtue and excuses faults.

Of English Verse

Poets may boast, as safely vain,
Their work shall with the world remain:
Both, bound together, live or die,
The verses and the prophecy.

But who can hope his lines should long
Last in a daily-changing tongue?
While they are new, envy prevails,
And as that dies, our language fails.

When architects have done their part,
10   The matter may betray their art;
Time, if we use ill-chosen stone,
Soon brings a well-built palace down.

Poets that lasting marble seek
Must carve in Latin or in Greek;
We write in sand; our language grows,
And like the tide our work o'erflows.

Chaucer his sense can only boast,
The glory of his numbers lost;
Years have defaced his matchless strain;
20   And yet he did not sing in vain.

The beauties which adorned that age,
The shining subjects of his rage,
Hoping they should immortal prove,
Rewarded with success his love.

This was the generous poet's scope,
And all an English pen can hope:
To make the fair approve his flame
That can so far extend their fame.

Verse thus designed has no ill fate,
30   If it arrive but at the date
Of fading beauty; if it prove
But as long-lived as present love.

Upon the Earl of Roscommon's Translation of Horace, De Arte Poetica
And of the Use of Poetry

Rome was not better by her Horace taught
Than we are here to comprehend his thought.
The poet writ to noble Piso there;
A noble Piso does instruct us here,
Gives us a pattern in his flowing style,
And with rich precepts does oblige our isle:
Britain, whose genius is in verse expressed:
Bold and sublime, but negligently dressed.
    Horace will our superfluous branches prune,
10 Give us new rules, and set our harp in tune;
Direct us how to back the wingèd horse,
Favour his flight, and moderate his force.
Though poets may of inspiration boast,
Their rage, ill-governed, in the clouds is lost.
He that proportioned wonders can disclose
At once his fancy and his judgment shows.
Chaste moral writing we may learn from hence,
Neglect of which no wit can recompense.
The fountain which from Helicon proceeds,
20 That sacred stream, should never water weeds,
Nor make the crop of thorns and thistles grow
Which Envy or perverted Nature sow.
    Well-sounding verses are the charm we use
Heroic thoughts and virtue to infuse;
Things of deep sense we may in prose unfold,
But they move more, in lofty numbers told.
By the loud trumpet, which our courage aids,
We learn that sound, as well as sense, persuades.
The Muses' friend, unto himself severe,
30 With silent pity looks on all that err;
But where a brave, a public action shines,
That he rewards with his immortal lines.
Whether it be in council or in fight,
His country's honour is his chief delight;

Praise of great acts he scatters as a seed
Which may the like in coming ages breed.
   Here taught the fate of verses (always prized
With admiration, or as much despised),
Men will be less indulgent to their faults,
40   And patience have to cultivate their thoughts.
Poets lose half the praise they should have got
Could it be known what they discreetly blot,
Finding new words, that to the ravished ear
May like the language of the gods appear –
Such as, of old, wise bards employed, to make
Unpolished men their wild retreats forsake;
Law-giving heroes, famed for taming brutes,
And raising cities with their charming lutes.
For rudest minds with harmony were caught,
50   And civil life was by the Muses taught.
So wandering bees would perish in the air,
Did not a sound, proportioned to their ear,
Appease their rage, invite them to the hive,
Unite their force, and teach them how to thrive,
To rob the flowers, and to forbear the spoil.
Preserved in winter by their summer's toil,
They give us food which may with nectar vie,
And wax that does the absent sun supply.

from *The New Masque for* The Maid's Tragedy

A Triton Sings
Love were too divine a blessing,
Could the happy minutes last;
Tides of pleasure, in possessing,
Sweetly flow but soon are past.
Take the full sea to befriend ye,
Fear no storm by the way,
No rock to offend ye,
But manfully steer for the bay.

Nereid

Gentle Night, befriend a lover
10 Long has had his bliss delayed,
Long has sighed thy watches over;
See him, see him now repaid.
Gentle Night, befriend a lover
Long has had his bliss delayed.

Thyrsis, eager for possessing,
Thinks the bride too long undressing;
When the innocent maid,
Of her wishes afraid,
Still delays though she longs for the blessing.
20 Thyrsis, eager for possessing,
Thinks the bride too long undressing.

Chorus

Love's a sweet but flitting treasure;
He that would secure the pleasure
Must watch to shoot the flying game.

Aeolus

Jolly bridegroom, take thy right;
Love and you must reign tonight.
Seize the virgin, boldly seize her;
Regard not her crying,
Her trembling and dying,
30 Deny what she begs and you please her.

Dance of Tritons and Sea-Nymphs

Sea-Nymph

Away with formal wooing,
While youth is in its prime;
Uncertain hopes pursuing
Is waste of love and time.
Away with formal wooing
While youth is in its prime.

Now, my shepherdess, be tender
While my love and life are warm;
Too late, alas, you will surrender
40   When I shall want the strength to storm.
Not a nymph that condoles you and pities your case,
But envies and wishes, but envies and wishes your place.

Chorus
Hymen, bring away the bride;
Lay her by her lover's side;
Night must give what day denied.

Of Tea, Commended by Her Majesty

Venus her myrtle, Phoebus has his bays;
Tea both excels, which she vouchsafes to praise.
The best of queens and best of herbs we owe
To that bold nation which the way did show
To the fair region where the sun does rise,
Whose rich productions we so justly prize.
The Muses' friend, Tea, does our fancy aid
Repress those vapours which the head invade,
And keeps that palace of the soul serene,
10   Fit on her birthday to salute the Queen.

Of the Last Verses in the Book

When we for age could neither read nor write,
The subject made us able to indite.
The soul, with nobler resolutions decked,
The body stooping, does herself erect:
No mortal parts are requisite to raise
Her that, unbodied, can her Maker praise.

The seas are quiet when the winds give o'er;
So calm are we, when passions are no more;
For then we know how vain it was to boast
10   Of fleeting things, so certain to be lost.
Clouds of affection from our younger eyes
Conceal that emptiness which age descries.

The soul's dark cottage, battered and decayed,
Lets in new light through chinks that time has made;
Stronger by weakness, wiser men become
As they draw near to their eternal home;
Leaving the old, both worlds at once they view
That stand upon the threshold of the new.

—*Miratur Limen Olympi.*
        Virgil

JOHN OLDHAM

SATIRES UPON THE JESUITS

from *Satire IV [Ignatius in Hell]*

These are the Fathers' implements and tools,
Their gaudy trangums for inveigling fools;
These serve for baits the simple to ensnare,
Like children spirited with toys at fair.
Nor are they half the artifices yet
By which the vulgar they delude and cheat:
Which should I undertake, much easier I
Much sooner might compute what sins there be
Wiped off and pardoned at a jubilee;
What bribes enrich the Datary each year,
Or vices treated on by Escobar;
How many whores in Rome profess the trade,
Or greater numbers by confession made.
    One undertakes by scale of miles to tell
The bounds, dimensions, and extent of Hell;
How far and wide th' infernal Monarch reigns,
How many German leagues his realm contains;
Who are his ministers pretends to know,
And all their several offices below;
How many cauldrons he each year expends
In coals for roasting Huguenots and fiends;
And with as much exactness states the case
As if he'd been surveyor of the place.
    Another frights the rout with rueful stories
Of wild Chimaeras, Limbos, Purgatories,
And bloated souls in smoky durance hung,
Like a Westphalia gammon or neat's tongue,
To be redeemed with masses and a song.
A good, round sum must the deliverance buy,
For none may there swear out on poverty.
Your rich and bounteous shades are only eased;
No Fleet or King's Bench ghosts are thence released.
    A third, the wicked and debauched to please,

10

20

30

Cries up the virtue of indulgences,
And all the rates of vices does assess;
What price they in the holy chamber bear,
And customs for each sin imported there;
How you at best advantages may buy
Patents for sacrilege and simony;
40   What tax is in the lechery-office laid
On pandars, bawds, and whores, that ply the trade;
What costs a rape or incest, and how cheap
You may an harlot or an ingle keep;
How easy murder may afforded be
For one, two, three, or a whole family
(But not of heretics: there no pardon lacks;
'Tis one o'th' Church's meritorious acts).

    For venial trifles, less and slighter faults,
They ne'er deserve the trouble of your thoughts.
50   Ten Ave Maries, mumbled to the Cross,
Clear scores of twice ten thousand such as those;
Some are at sound of christened bell forgiven,
And some by squirt of holy water driven;
Others by anthem played are charmed away,
As men cure bites of the tarantula.

    But nothing with the crowd does more enhance
The value of these holy charlatans
Than when the wonders of the mass they view,
Where spiritual jugglers their chief mastery show:
60   'Hey Jingo, Sirs!' What's this? 'Tis bread you see;
'Presto, be gone!' 'Tis now a deity.
Two grains of dough, with cross and stamp of priest
And five small words pronounced, make up their Christ.
To this they all fall down, this all adore,
And straight devour what they adored before;
Down goes the tiny Saviour at a bit,
To be digested, and at length beshit;
From altar to close stool or jakes preferred,
First wafer, next a God, and then a turd.

A Letter from the Country to a Friend in Town
Giving an Account of the Author's Inclinations to Poetry.
Written in July, 1678

As, to that poet (if so great a one as he
May suffer in comparison with me),
When, heretofore in Scythian exile pent,
To which he by ungrateful Rome was sent,
If a kind paper from his country came,
And wore, subscribed, some known and faithful name:
That, like a powerful cordial, did infuse
New life into his speechless, gasping Muse,
And straight his genius, which before did seem
10   Bound up in ice and frozen as the clime,
By its warm force and friendly influence, thawed,
Dissolved apace, and in soft numbers flowed;
Such welcome here, dear Sir, your letter had
With me, shut up in close constraint as bad.
Not eager lovers, held in long suspense,
With warmer joy and a more tender sense
Meet those kind lines which all their wishes bless,
And sign and seal delivered Happiness.
My grateful thoughts so throng to get abroad,
20   They overrun each other in the crowd;
To you with hasty flight they take their way,
And hardly for the dress of words will stay.
    Yet pardon, if this only fault I find,
That while you praise too much, you are less kind.
Consider, Sir: 'tis ill and dangerous thus
To over-lay a young and tender Muse.
Praise, the fine diet, which we're apt to love,
If given to excess, does hurtful prove;
Where it does weak, distempered stomachs meet,
30   That surfeits which should nourishment create.
Your rich perfumes such fragrancy dispense,
Their sweetness overcomes and palls my sense;
On my weak head you heap so many bays,
I sink beneath 'em, quite oppressed with praise,

And a resembling fate with him receive
Who in too kind a triumph found his grave,
Smothered with garlands which applauders gave.
  To you these praises justlier all belong,
By alienating which, yourself you wrong:
40 Whom better can such commendations fit
Than you, who so well teach and practise Wit?
Verse, the great boast of drudging fools, from some,
Nay most, of scribblers with much straining come;
They void 'em dribbling and in pain they write,
As if they had a strangury of wit.
Your pen, uncalled, they readily obey,
And scorn your ink should flow so fast as they;
Each strain of yours so easy does appear,
Each such a graceful negligence does wear,
50 As shows you have none and yet want no care.
None of your serious pains or time they cost,
But what, thrown by, you can afford for lost.
If such the fruits of your loose leisure be,
Your careless minutes yield such poetry,
We guess what proofs your genius would impart
Did it employ you, as it does divert.
But happy you, more prudent and more wise,
With better aims have fixed your noble choice;
While silly I all thriving arts refuse,
60 And all my hopes and all my vigour lose
In service on that worst of jilts, a Muse;
For gainful business court ignoble ease,
And in gay trifles waste my ill-spent days.
  Little I thought, my dearest friend, that you
Would thus contribute to my ruin too.
O'errun with filthy poetry and rhyme,
The present reigning evil of the time,
I lacked, and (well I did myself assure)
From your kind hand I should receive, a cure:
70 When, lo, instead of healing remedies,
You cherish and encourage the disease;
Inhumane, you help the distemper on,
Which was before but too inveterate grown.

As a kind looker-on, who interest shares,
Though not in's stake, yet in his hopes and fears,
Would to his friend, a pushing gamester, do –
Recall his elbow when he hastes to throw;
Such a wise course you should have took with me,
A rash and vent'ring fool in poetry.

80   Poets are cullies whom rook Fame draws in,
And wheedles with deluding hopes to win;
But, when they hit and most successful are,
They scarce come off with a bare saving share.

   Oft, I remember, did wise friends dissuade,
And bid me quit the trifling, barren trade;
Oft have I tried (Heav'n knows) to mortify
This vile and wicked lust of poetry;
But, still unconquered, it remains within,
Fixed as an habit or some darling sin.

90   In vain I better studies there would sow:
Often I've tried, but none will thrive or grow.
All my best thoughts, when I'd most serious be,
Are never from its foul infection free;
Nay (God forgive me!) when I say my prayers,
Scarce can help polluting them with verse.
That fabulous wretch of old, reversed, I seem,
Who turn whate'er I touch to dross and rhyme.

   Oft, to divert the wild caprice, I try
If sovereign wisdom and philosophy,
100   Rightly applied, will give a remedy.
Straight the great Stagyrite I take in hand,
Seek Nature and myself to understand;
Much I reflect on his vast worth and fame,
And much my low and grovelling aims condemn,
And quarrel that my ill-packed fate should be
This vain, this worthless thing called poetry.
But when I find this unregarded toy
Could his important thoughts and pains employ,
By reading there I am but more undone,
110   And meet that danger which I went to shun.

Oft when ill-humour, chagrin, discontent
Give leisure my wild follies to resent,
I thus against myself my passion vent.
'Enough, mad, rhyming sot; enough for shame;
Give o'er, and all thy quills to tooth-picks damn;
Didst ever thou the altar rob, or worse,
Kill the priest there and maids receiving force?
What else could merit this so heavy curse?
The greatest curse I can I wish on him
120 (If there be any greater than to rhyme)
Who first did of the lewd invention think;
First made two lines with sounds resembling clink,
And, swerving from the easy paths of prose,
Fetters and chains did on free sense impose.
Curst too be all the fools who since have went,
Misled, in steps of that ill precedent:
Want be entailed their lot' – and on I go,
Wreaking my spite on all the juggling crew;
Scarce the beloved Cowley 'scapes (though I
130 Might sooner my own curses fear than he);
And, thus resolved against the scribbling vein,
I deeply swear never to write again.

But when bad company and wine conspire
To kindle and renew the foolish fire,
Straightways relapsed, I feel the raving fit
Return, and straight I all my oaths forget;
The spirit, which I thought cast out before,
Enters again with stronger force and power,
Worse than at first, and tyrannizes more.
140 No sober, good advice will then prevail,
Or from the raging frenzy me recall;
Cool Reason's dictates me no more can move
Than men in drink, in Bedlam, or in love;
Deaf to all means which might most proper seem
Towards my cure, I run stark mad in rhyme,
A sad, poor, haunted wretch, whom nothing less
Than prayers of the Church can dispossess.

Sometimes, after a tedious day half-spent,
When Fancy long has hunted on cold scent,

150 Tired in the dull and fruitless chase of Thought,
  Despairing, I grow weary and give out.
  As a dry lecher, pumped of all my store,
  I loathe the thing 'cause I can do 't no more.
  But when I once begin to find again
  Recruits of matter in my pregnant brain,
  Again, more eager, I the haunt pursue,
  And with fresh vigour the loved sport renew;
  Tickled with some strange pleasure, which I find,
  And think a secrecy to all mankind,
160 I please myself with the vain, false delight,
  And count none happy but the fops that write.
   'Tis endless, Sir, to tell the many ways
  Wherein my poor, deluded self I please:
  How when the Fancy, labouring for a birth,
  With unfelt throes brings its rude issue forth;
  How after, when imperfect, shapeless thought
  Is by the Judgment into fashion wrought.
  When at first search I traverse o'er my mind,
  Nought but a dark and empty void I find.
170 Some little hints at length, like sparks, break thence,
  And glimmering thoughts just dawning into sense.
  Confused awhile the mixed ideas lie,
  With nought of mark to be discovered by,
  Like colours, undistinguished in the night,
  Till the dusk images, moved to the light,
  Teach the discerning faculty to choose
  Which it had best adopt and which refuse.
  Here, rougher strokes, touched with a careless dash,
  Resemble the first sitting of a face;
180 There, finished drafts in form more full appear,
  And to their justness ask no further care.
  Meanwhile, with inward joy, I proud am grown
  To see the work successfully go on,
  And prize myself in a creating power
  That could make something what was nought before.
   Sometimes a stiff, unwieldy thought I meet
  Which to my laws will scarce be made submit,

But when, after expense of pains and time,
'Tis managed well and taught to yoke in rhyme,
190 I triumph more than joyful warriors would
Had they some stout and hardy foe subdued;
And idly think less goes to their command,
That makes armed troops in well-placed order stand,
Than to the conduct of my words, when they
March in due ranks, are set in just array.
    Sometimes, on wings of thought, I seem on high,
As men in sleep, though motionless they lie,
Fledged by a dream, believe they mount and fly;
So witches some enchanted wand bestride,
200 And think they through the airy regions ride
Where Fancy is both traveller, way, and guide.
Then straight I grow a strange, exalted thing,
And equal, in conceit, at least a king;
As the poor drunkard, when wine stums his brains,
Anointed with that liquor, thinks he reigns.
Bewitched by these delusions 'tis I write
(The tricks some pleasant devil plays in spite),
And when I'm in the freakish trance, which I
(Fond, silly wretch) mistake for ecstasy,
210 I find all former resolutions vain,
And thus recant them, and make new again.
    'What was't I rashly vowed? Shall ever I
Quit my beloved mistress, Poetry?
Thou sweet beguiler of my lonely hours,
Which thus glide unperceived with silent course;
Thou gentle spell, which undisturbed dost keep
My breast, and charm intruding Care asleep!
They say thou'rt poor and unendowed: what though?
For thee I this vain, worthless world forgo.
220 Let wealth and honour be for Fortune's slaves,
The alms of fools and prize of crafty knaves;
To me thou art whate'er the ambitious crave,
And all that greedy misers want or have.
In youth or age, in travel or at home,
Here or in town, at London or at Rome,

Rich or a beggar, free or in the Fleet,
Whate'er my fate is, 'tis my fate to write.'
   Thus I have made my shrifted Muse confess
Her secret feebles and her weaknesses;
230 All her hid faults she sets exposed to view,
And hopes a gentle confessor in you;
She hopes an easy pardon for her sin,
Since 'tis but what she is not wilful in,
Nor yet has scandalous nor open been.
Try if your ghostly counsel can reclaim
The heedless wanton from her guilt and shame;
At least be not ungenerous, to reproach
That wretched frailty which you've helped debauch.
   'Tis now high time to end, for fear I grow
240 More tedious than old doters when they woo,
Than travelled fops when far-fetched lies they prate,
Or flattering poets when they dedicate.
No dull forgiveness I presume to crave,
Nor vainly for my tiresome length ask leave,
Lest I, as often formal coxcombs use,
Prolong that very fault I would excuse.
May this the same kind welcome find with you
As yours did here, and ever shall; adieu.

Upon a Printer that Exposed him
Printing a Piece of His Grossly Mangled and Faulty

Dull and unthinking! Hadst thou none but me
To plague and urge to thine own infamy?
Had I some tame and sneaking author been,
Whose Muse to love and softness did incline;
Some small adventurer in song, that whines
'Chloris' and 'Phyllis' out in charming lines,
Fit to divert Mine Hostess, and mislead
The heart of some poor tawdry waiting-maid;
Perhaps I might have then forgiven thee,
10 And thou hadst 'scaped from my resentments free.

But I, whom spleen and manly rage inspire,
Brook no affront, at each offence take fire;
Born to chastise the vices of the age,
Which pulpits dare not, nor the very stage;
Sworn to lash knaves of all degrees, and spare
None of the kind, however great they are;
Satire's my only province and delight,
For whose dear sake alone I've vowed to write.
For this I seek occasions, court abuse,
20   To show my parts and signalize my Muse;
Fond of a quarrel as young bullies are
To make their mettle and their skill appear.
And didst thou think I would a wrong acquit,
That touched my tender'st part of honour, Wit?
No, villain: may my sins ne'er pardoned be
By Heav'n itself, if e'er I pardon thee.
  Members from breach of privilege deter
By threatening Topham and a messenger;
Scroggs and the Brothers of the Coif oppose
30   The force and dint of statutes and the laws;
Strumpets of Billingsgate redress their wrongs
By the sole noise and foulness of their tongues;
And I go always armed for my defence,
To punish and revenge an insolence.
I wear my pen, as others do their sword;
To each affronting sot I meet, the word
Is 'Satisfaction!'; straight to thrusts I go,
And pointed satire runs him through and through.
  Perhaps thou hoped'st that thy obscurity
40   Should be thy safeguard and secure thee free;
No, wretch: I mean from thence to fetch thee out,
Like sentenced felons, to be dragged about;
Torn, mangled, and exposed to scorn and shame,
I mean to hang and gibbet up thy name.
If thou to live in satire so much thirst,
Enjoy thy wish and fame till envy burst,
Renowned as he whom banished Ovid cursed;
Or he whom old Archilochus so stung
In verse, that he for shame and madness hung.

50   Deathless in infamy, do thou so live,
      And let my rage, like his, to halters drive.
         Thou thought'st perhaps my gall was spent and gone,
      My venom drained, and I a senseless drone;
      Thou thought'st I had no curses left in store;
      But to thy sorrow know and find I've more,
      More, and more dreadful yet, able to scare
      Like Hell, and urge to daggers and despair;
      Such, thou shalt feel, are still reserved by me
      To vex and force thee to thy destiny.
60   Since thou hast braved my vengeance thus, prepare,
      And tremble from my pen thy doom to hear.
         Thou, who with spurious nonsense durst profane
      The genuine issue of a poet's brain,
      May'st thou hereafter never deal in verse,
      But what hoarse bellmen in their walks rehearse,
      Or Smithfield audience sung on crickets hears.
      May'st thou print Howard, or some duller ass:
      Jordan, or him that wrote *Dutch Hudibras*;
      Or next vile scribbler of the house, whose play
70   Will scarce for candles and their snuffing pay.
      May you each other curse; thyself undone,
      And he the laughing-stock of all the town.
         May'st thou ne'er rise to history, but what
      Poor Grubstreet penny-chronicles relate:
      Memoirs of Tyburn, and the mournful state
      Of cut-purses in Holborn cavalcade;
      Till thou thyself be the same subject made.
      Compelled by want, may'st thou print Popery,
      For which be the cart's arse and pillory,
80   Turnips and rotten eggs thy destiny;
      Mauled worse than Reading, Christian, or Cellier,
      Till thou, daubed o'er with loathsome filth, appear
      Like brat of some vile drab in privy found,
      Which there has lain three months in ordure drowned.
         The plague of poets, rags and poetry,
      Debts, writs, arrest, and sergeants light on thee;
      For others bound, may'st thou to durance go,
      Condemned to scraps and begging with a shoe;

And may'st thou never from the jail get free,
90   Till thou swear out thyself by perjury;
Forlorn, abandoned, pitiless, and poor,
As a pawned cully or a mortgaged whore,
May'st thou an halter want for thy redress,
Forced to steal hemp to end thy miseries,
And damn thyself to baulk the hangman's fees.
    And may no saucy fool have better fate,
      That dares pull down the vengeance of my hate.

Imitation of Horace. Book I, Satire IX
Written in June, 1681

As I was walking in the Mall of late,
Alone and musing on I know not what,
Comes a familiar fop, whom hardly I
Knew by his name, and rudely seizes me:
'Dear Sir, I'm mighty glad to meet with you!
And pray, how have you done, this age or two?'
'Well, I thank God,' I said, 'as times are now;
I wish the same to you.' And so passed on,
Hoping with this the coxcomb would be gone.
10   But when I saw I could not thus get free,
I asked what business else he had with me.
'Sir,' answered he, 'if learning, parts, or sense
Merit your friendship, I have just pretence.'
'I honour you,' said I, 'upon that score,
And shall be glad to serve you to my power.'
Meantime, wild to get loose, I try all ways
To shake him off: sometimes I walk apace,
Sometimes stand still; I frown, I chafe, I fret,
Shrug, turn my back; as in the Bagnio, sweat;
20   And show all kind of signs to make him guess
At my impatience and uneasiness.
'Happy the folk in Newgate,' whispered I,
'Who, though in chains, are from this torment free!

Would I were like rough Manly in the play,
To send impertinents with kicks away!'
   He all the while baits me with tedious chat,
Speaks much about the drought, and how the rate
Of hay is raised, and what it now goes at;
Tells me of a new comet at the Hague,
30   Portending God knows what – a dearth, or plague;
Names every wench that passes through the Park,
How much she is allowed, and who the spark
That keeps her; points, who lately got a clap,
And who at the Groom-Porter's had ill hap
Three nights ago in play with such a lord.
When he observed I minded not a word,
And did no answer to his trash afford,
'Sir, I perceive you stand on thorns,' said he,
'And fain would part; but, faith, it must not be;
40   Come, let us take a bottle.' I cried, 'No!
Sir, I am in a course, and dare not now.'
'Then tell me whither you design to go;
I'll wait upon you.' 'Oh Sir, 'tis too far;
I visit 'cross the water; therefore spare
Your needless trouble.' 'Trouble! Sir, 'tis none;
'Tis more by half to leave you here alone.
I have no present business to attend,
At least which I'll not quit for such a friend.
Tell me not of the distance, for I vow
50   I'll cut the Line, double the Cape for you;
Good faith, I will not leave you; make no words.
Go you to Lambeth? Is it to My Lord's?
His steward I most intimately know,
Have often drunk with his comptroller too.'
By this I found my wheedle would not pass,
But rather served my sufferings to increase;
And seeing 'twas in vain to vex or fret,
I patiently submitted to my fate.
   Straight he begins again: 'Sir, if you knew
60   My worth but half so throughly as I do,
I'm sure you would not value any friend
You have, like me; but that I won't commend

Myself and my own talents, I might tell
How many ways to wonder I excel.
None has a greater gift in poetry,
Or writes more verses with more ease than I;
I'm grown the envy of the men of wit:
I killed ev'n Rochester with grief and spite.
Next, for the dancing part I all surpass:
70   St André never moved with such a grace;
And 'tis well known, whene'er I sing or set,
Humphreys nor Blow could ever match me yet.'
    Here I got room to interrupt: 'Have you
A mother, Sir, or kindred living now?'
'Not one; they are all dead.' 'Troth, so I guessed:
The happier they,' said I, 'who are at rest.
Poor I am only left unmurdered yet;
Haste, I beseech you, and dispatch me quite,
For I am well convinced my time is come.
80   When I was young, a gipsy told my doom:
"This lad," said she, and looked upon my hand,
"Shall not by sword or poison come to's end,
Nor by the fever, dropsy, gout, or stone,
But he shall die by an eternal Tongue;
Therefore, when he's grown up, if he be wise,
Let him avoid great talkers I advise."'
    By this time we were got to Westminster,
Where he by chance a trial had to hear,
And if he were not there, his cause must fall.
90   'Sir, if you love me, step into the Hall
For one half hour.' 'The Devil take me now,'
Said I, 'if I know anything of law;
Besides I told you whither I'm to go.'
Hereat he made a stand, pulled down his hat
Over his eyes, and mused in deep debate.
'I'm in a strait,' said he, 'what I shall do;
Whether forsake my business, Sir, or you.'
'Me, by all means,' say I. 'No,' says my sot;
'I fear you'll take it ill, if I should do't;
100 I'm sure you will.' 'Not I, by all that's good.'
'But I've more breeding than to be so rude.'

'Pray, don't neglect your own concerns for me;
Your cause, good Sir!' 'My cause be damned,' says he;
'I value't less than your dear company.'
With this he came up to me, and would lead
The way; I, sneaking after, hung my head.
   Next he begins to plague me with the Plot:
Asks whether I were known to Oates or not.
'Not I, thank Heaven! I no priest have been;
Have never Douai nor St Omers seen.'
'What think you, Sir? Will they Fitzharris try?
Will he die, think you?' 'Yes, most certainly.'
'I mean, be hanged.' 'Would thou were so,' wished I.
Religion came in next – though he'd no more
Than the French king, his punk, or confessor.
'Oh, the sad times, if once the King should die!
Sir, are you not afraid of popery?'
'No more than my superiors; why should I?
I've no estate in abbey-lands to lose.'
'But fire and faggot, Sir, how like you those?'
'Come, Inquisition, anything,' thought I,
'So Heav'n would bless me to get rid of thee!
But 'tis some comfort that my Hell is here;
I need no punishment hereafter fear.'
   Scarce had I thought, but he falls on anew.
'How stands it, Sir, betwixt His Grace and you?'
'Sir, he's a man of sense above the crowd,
And shuns the converse of a multitude.'
'Aye, Sir,' says he, 'you're happy, who are near
His Grace, and have the favour of his ear;
But let me tell you, if you'll recommend
This person here, your point will soon be gained.
Gad, Sir, I'll die, if my own single wit
Don't fob his minions, and displace 'em quite,
And make yourself his only favourite.'
'No, you are out abundantly,' said I;
'We live not as you think; no family
Throughout the whole three kingdoms is more free
From those ill customs which are used to swarm
In great men's houses; none e'er does me harm

110

120

130

140

Because more learned or more rich than I,
But each man keeps his place and his degree.'
''Tis mighty strange,' says he, 'what you relate.'
'But nothing truer, take my word for that.'
'You make me long to be admitted too
Amongst his creatures. Sir, I beg that you
Will stand my friend; your interest is such,
You may prevail, I'm sure; you can do much.
He's one that may be won upon, I've heard,
150   Though at the first approach access be hard.
I'll spare no trouble of my own, or friends',
No cost in fees and bribes to gain my ends;
I'll seek all opportunites to meet
With him, accost him in the very street;
Hang on his coach and wait upon him home,
Fawn, scrape, and cringe to him, nay to his groom.
Faith, Sir, this must be done, if we'll be great:
Preferment comes not a cheaper rate.'
        While at this savage rate he worried me,
160   By chance a doctor, my dear friend, came by,
That knew the fellow's humour passing well.
Glad of the sight, I join him; we stand still.
'Whence came you, Sir? And whither go you now?'
And such like questions passed betwixt us two.
Straight I begin to pull him by the sleeve,
Nod, wink upon him, touch my nose, and give
A thousand hints to let him know that I
Needed his help for my delivery.
He, naughty wag, with an arch, fleering smile
170   Seems ignorant of what I mean the while.
I grow stark wild with rage. 'Sir, said not you
You'd somewhat to discourse, not long ago,
With me in private?' 'I remember't well;
Some other time, be sure, I will not fail.
Now I am in great haste, upon my word;
A messenger came for me from a lord
That's in a bad condition, like to die.'
'Oh Sir, he can't be in a worse than I;

Therefore for God's sake do not stir from hence.'
180 'Sweet Sir, your pardon; 'tis of consequence;
I hope you're kinder than to press my stay,
Which may be Heav'n knows what out of my way.'
This said, he left me to my murderer.
Seeing no hopes of my relief appear,
'Confounded be the stars,' said I, 'that swayed
This fatal day! Would I had kept my bed
With sickness, rather than been visited
With this worse plague! What ill have I e'er done
To pull this curse, this heavy judgment down?'
190   While I was thus lamenting my ill hap,
Comes aid at length: a brace of bailiffs clap
The rascal on the back. 'Here take your fees,
Kind gentlemen,' said I, 'for my release.'
He would have had me bail. 'Excuse me, Sir,
I've made a vow ne'er to be surety more;
My father was undone by't heretofore.'
    Thus I got off, and blessed the Fates that he
    Was prisoner made, I set at liberty.

A Satire upon a Woman
Who, by her Falsehood and Scorn, was the Death of his Friend

No, she shall ne'er escape, if gods there be,
Unless they perjured grow and false as she.
Though no strange judgment yet the murderess seize,
To punish her and 'quit the partial skies;
Though no revenging lightning yet has flashed
From thence, that might her criminal beauties blast;
Though they in their old lustre still prevail,
By no disease, nor guilt itself, made pale
(Guilt which, should blackest Moors themselves but own,
10 Would make, through all their night, new blushes dawn);
Though that kind soul, who now augments the Blest,
Thither too soon by her unkindness chased

(Where may it be her small'st and lightest doom –
For that's not half my curse – never to come);
Though he, when prompted by the highest despair,
Ne'er mentioned her without a hymn or prayer,
And could by all her scorn be forced no more
Than martyrs to revile what they adore –
Who, had he cursed her with his dying breath,
Had done but just, and Heaven had forgave;
Though ill-made law no sentence has ordained
For her, no statute has her guilt arraigned
(For hangmen, women's scorn, and doctor's skill,
All by a licensed way of murder kill);
Though she from justice of all these go free,
And boast perhaps in her success, and cry,
' 'Twas but a little harmless perjury';
Yet think she not she still secure shall prove,
Or that none dare avenge an injured love.
I rise in judgment, am to be to her
Both witness, judge, and executioner;
Armed with dire satire and resentful spite,
I come to haunt her with the ghosts of Wit.
My ink, unbid, starts out and flies on her
Like blood upon some touching murderer;
And should that fail, rather than want, I would
(Like hags) to curse her, write in my own blood.
    Ye spiteful powers (if any there can be
That boast a worse and keener spite than I),
Assist with malice and your mighty aid
My sworn revenge, and help me rhyme her dead;
Grant I may fix such brands of infamy,
So plain, so deeply graved on her, that she,
Her skill, patches, nor paint, all joined, can hide,
And which shall lasting as her soul abide;
Grant my rank hate may such strong poison cast
That every breath may taint, and rot, and blast,
Till one large gangrene quite o'erspread her fame
With foul contagion; till her odious name,
Spit at and cursed by every mouth like mine,
Be terror to herself and all her line.

20

30

40

50

    Vil'st of that viler sex who damned us all!
Ordained to cause, and plague us for, our Fall!
Woman! Nay, worse! For she can nought be said
But mummy by some devil inhabited;
Not made in Heaven's mint, but basely coined,
She wears an human image stamped on fiend,
And whoso marriage would with her contract
Is witch by law, and that a mere compact;
60 Her soul (if any soul in her there be)
By Hell was breathed into her in a lie,
And its whole stock of falsehood there was lent,
As if hereafter to be true it meant;
Bawd Nature taught her jilting when she made,
And by her make designed her for the trade;
Hence 'twas she daubed her with a painted face,
That she at once might better cheat and please.
All those gay, charming looks that court the eye
Are but an ambush to hid treachery;
70 Mischief adorned with pomp and smooth disguise,
A painted skin stuffed full of guile and lies,
Within a gawdy case a nasty soul,
Like turds of quality in a gilt close-stool.
Such on a cloud those flattering colours are
Which only serve to dress a tempest fair.
So men upon this earth's fair surface dwell;
Within are fiends, and at the centre, Hell.
Court-promises, the leagues which statesmen make
With more convenience and more ease to break,
80 The faith a Jesuit in allegiance swears,
Or a town-jilt to keeping coxcombs bears,
Are firm and certain all, compared with hers.
Early in falsehood, at her font she lied,
And should ev'n then for perjury been tried;
Her conscience, stretched and open as the stews,
But laughs at oaths and plays with solemn vows,
And at her mouth swallows down perjured breath,
More glib than bits of lechery beneath.
Less serious known when she doth most protest
90 Than thoughts of arrantest buffoons in jest;

More cheap than the vile, mercenariest squire,
That plies for half-crown fees at Westminster,
And trades in staple oaths, and swears to hire;
Less guilt than hers, less breach of oath and word
Has stood aloft and looked through penance-board;
And he that trusts her in a death-bed prayer
Has faith to merit and save anything, but her.
　　But since her guilt description does outgo,
I'll try if it outstrip my curses too:
100　Curses which, may they equal my just hate,
My wish, and her desert; be each so great,
Each heard like prayers, and Heaven make 'em Fate!
　　First, for her beauties, which the mischief brought:
May she affected, they be borrowed, thought,
By her own hand, not that of Nature, wrought.
Her credit, honour, portion, health, and those,
Prove light and frail as her broke faith and vows;
Some base, unnamed disease her carcass foul,
And make her body ugly as her soul;
110　Cankers and ulcers eat her, till she be
Shunned like infection, loathed like infamy;
Strength quite expired, may she alone retain
The snuff of life; may that unquenched remain,
As in the damned, to keep her fresh for pain;
Hot Lust light on her, and the plague of Pride
On that – this ever scorned, as that denied;
Ache, Anguish, Horror, Grief, Dishonour, Shame
Pursue at once her body, soul, and fame;
If e'er the devil Love must enter her
120　(For nothing sure but fiends can enter there)
May she a just and true tormenter find,
And that like an ill conscience rack her mind;
Be some diseased and ugly wretch her fate,
She doomed to love of one whom all else hate.
May he hate her, and may her destiny
Be to despair, and yet love on, and die;
Or (to invent some wittier punishment)
May he, to plague her, out of spite consent;

      May the old fumbler, though disabled quite,
130   Have strength to give her claps but no delight;
      May he of her unjustly jealous be
      For one that's worse and uglier far than he;
      May 's impotence balk and torment her lust,
      Yet scarcely her to dreams or wishes trust;
      Forced to be chaste, may she suspected be;
      Share none o'th'pleasure, all the infamy.
        In fine, that I all curses may complete
      (For I've but cursed in jest and rallied yet):
      Whate'er the sex deserves, or feels, or fears,
140   May all those plagues be hers, and only hers;
      Whate'er great favourites turned out of doors,
      Scorned lovers, bilked and disappointed whores,
      Or losing gamesters, vent; what curses e'er
      Are spoke by sinners raving in despair;
      All those fall on her, as they're all her due,
      Till Spite can't think, nor Heav'n inflict anew.
      May then (for once I will be kind and pray)
      No madness take her use of sense away,
      But may she in full strength of reason be,
150   To feel and understand her misery;
      Plagued so, till she think damning a release,
      And humbly pray to go to Hell for ease;
      Yet may not all these sufferings here atone
      Her sin, and may she still go sinning on,
      Tick up in perjury, and run o'th'score,
      Till on her soul she can get trust no more.
        Then may she, stupid and repentless, die,
        And Heav'n itself forgive no more than I,
        But so be damned of mere necessity.

Catullus, Epigram VII, Imitated

Quaeris quot mihi basiationes . . .

Nay, Lesbia, never ask me this,
'How many kisses will suffice?'
Faith, 'tis a question hard to tell,
Exceeding hard; for you as well
May ask what sums of gold suffice
The greedy miser's boundless wish.
Think what drops the ocean store,
With all the sands that make its shore;
Think what spangles deck the skies
10   When Heaven looks with all its eyes;
Or think how many atoms came
To compose this mighty frame.
Let all these the counters be
To tell how oft I'm kissed by thee,
Till no malicious spy can guess
To what vast height the scores arise;
Till weak arithmetic grow scant
And numbers for the reckoning want.
All these will hardly be enough
20   For me, stark staring mad with love.

A Fragment of Petronius, Paraphrased

Foeda est in coitu, & brevis voluptas, &c.

I hate fruition, now 'tis past:
'Tis all but nastiness at best;
The homeliest thing that man can do;
Besides, 'tis short and fleeting too.
A squirt of slippery delight
That with a moment takes its flight;

A fulsome bliss that soon does cloy
And makes us loathe what we enjoy.
Then let us not too eager run,
10 By passion blindly hurried on,
Like beasts, who nothing better know
That what mere lust incites them to;
For when in floods of love we're drenched,
The flames are by enjoyment quenched.
But thus, let's thus together lie
And kiss out long eternity,
Where we dread no conscious spies,
No blushes stain our guiltless joys;
Here no faintness dulls desires
20 And pleasure never flags nor tires;
This has pleased, and pleases now,
And for ages will do so.
    Enjoyment here is never done,
    But fresh, and always but begun.

An Ode of Anacreon Paraphrased: The Cup

Make me a bowl, a mighty bowl,
Large as my capacious soul,
Vast as my thirst is; let it have
Depth enough to be my grave –
I mean the grave of all my care,
For I intend to bury't there.
Let it of silver fashioned be,
Worthy of wine, worthy of me,
Worthy to adorn the spheres,
10 As that bright Cup amongst the stars:
That Cup which Heaven deigned a place,
Next the sun its greatest grace;
Kind Cup, that to the stars did go
To light poor drunkards here below!
Let mine be so, and give me light
That I may drink and revel by't.

Yet draw no shapes of armour there,
No cask, nor shield, nor sword, nor spear,
Nor wars of Thebes, nor wars of Troy,
20 Nor any other martial toy;
For what do I vain armour prize,
Who mind not such rough exercise,
But gentler sieges, softer wars,
Fights that cause no wounds or scars?
I'll have no battles on my plate,
Lest sight of them should brawls create;
Lest that provoke to quarrels too,
Which wine itself enough can do.
Draw me no constellations there,
30 No Ram, nor Bull, nor Dog, nor Bear,
Nor any of that monstrous fry
Of animals which stock the sky;
For what are stars to my design,
Stars, which I, when drunk, outshine,
Outshone by every drop of wine?
I lack no Pole Star on the brink
To guide in the wide sea of drink,
But would for ever there be tossed,
And wish no haven, seek no coast.
40 Yet, gentle artist, if thou'lt try
Thy skill, then draw me (let me see):
Draw me first a spreading vine;
Make its arms the bowl entwine
With kind embraces, such as I
Twist about my loving she;
Let its boughs o'erspread above
Scenes of drinking, scenes of love.
Draw next the patron of that tree:
Draw Bacchus and soft Cupid by;
50 Draw them both in toping shapes,
Their temples crowned with clustered grapes;
Make them lean against the cup
As 'twere to keep their figures up;

And when their reeling forms I view,
I'll think them drunk, and be so too.
  The gods shall my examples be;
  The gods, thus drunk in effigy.

An Allusion to Martial. Book I, Epigram 118

As oft, Sir Tradewell, as we meet,
You're sure to ask me, in the street,
When you shall send your boy to me
To fetch my book of poetry,
And promise you'll but read it o'er
And faithfully the loan restore.
But let me tell ye, as a friend,
You need not take the pains to send:
'Tis a long way to where I dwell,
At farther end of Clerkenwell;
There, in a garret near the sky,
Above five pair of stairs I lie.
But if you'd have what you pretend,
You may procure it nearer hand:
In Cornhill, where you often go,
Hard by th'Exchange, there is, you know,
A shop of rhyme, where you may see
The posts all clad in poetry.
There Hindmarsh lives, of high renown,
The noted'st Tory in the town;
Where, if you please, enquire for me,
And he or's prentice presently
From the next shelf will reach you down
The piece, well bound, for half a crown.
'The price is much too dear,' you cry,
'To give for both' – the book and me.
Yes, doubtless; for such vanities,
We know, Sir, you are too, too wise.

A Satire Addressed to a Friend
*That is about to Leave the University and come Abroad
in the World*

If you're so out of love with happiness
To quit a college-life and learned ease,
Convince me first, and some good reasons give,
What methods and designs you'll take to live.
For such resolves are needful in the case,
Before you tread the world's mysterious maze;
Without the premisses, in vain you'll try
To live by systems of philosophy;
Your Aristotle, Cartes, and Le Grand,
10   And Euclid too, in little stead will stand.
     How many men of choice and noted parts,
Well fraught with learning, languages, and arts,
Designing high preferment in their mind
And little doubting good success to find,
With vast and towering thoughts have flocked to town,
But to their cost soon found themselves undone,
Now to repent and starve at leisure left,
Of misery's last comfort, Hope, bereft?
     'These failed for want of good advice,' you cry,
20   'Because at first they fixed on no employ.'
Well then, let's draw the prospect and the scene
To all advantage possibly we can.
The world lies now before you: let me hear
What course your judgment counsels you to steer –
Always considered that your whole estate,
And all your fortune, lies beneath your hat.
Were you the son of some rich usurer,
That starved and damned himself to make his heir
Left nought to do but to inter the sot,
30   And spend with ease what *he* with pains had got,
'Twere easy to advise how you might live,
Nor would there need instruction then to give.
But you, that boast of no inheritance,
Save that small stock which lies within your brains:

Learning must be your trade, and therefore weigh
With heed how you your game the best may play;
Bethink yourself awhile, and then propose
What way of life is fitt'st for you to choose.
    If you for orders and a gown design,
40   Consider only this, dear friend of mine:
The Church is grown so overstocked of late
That if you walk abroad you'll hardly meet
More porters now than parsons in the street.
At every corner they are forced to ply
For jobs of hawkering divinity,
And half the number of the sacred herd
Are fain to stroll and wander, unpreferred.
    If this, or thoughts of such a weighty charge,
Make you resolve to keep yourself at large,
50   For want of better opportunity
A school must your next sanctuary be.
Go, wed some grammar-Bridewell and a wife,
And there beat Greek and Latin for your life;
With birchen sceptre there command at will,
Greater than Busby's self, or Doctor Gill.
But who would be to the vile drudgery bound,
Where there so small encouragement is found?
Where you, for recompence of all your pains,
Shall hardly reach a common fiddler's gains?
60   For when you've toiled and laboured all you can
To dung and cultivate a barren brain,
A dancing-master shall be better paid,
Though he instructs the heels and you the head.
To such indulgence are kind parents grown
That nought costs less in breeding than a son;
Nor is it hard to find a father now
Shall more upon a setting-dog allow,
And with a freer hand reward the care
Of training up his spaniel, than his heir.
70   Some think themselves exalted to the sky
If they light in some noble family:
Diet, a horse, and thirty pounds a year,
Besides th'advantage of His Lordship's ear,

The credit of the business and the State,
Are things that in a youngster's sense sound great.
Little the unexperienced wretch does know
What slavery he oft must undergo;
Who, though in silken scarf and cassock dressed,
Wears but a gayer livery at best.

80   When dinner calls, the implement must wait
With holy words to consecrate the meat,
But hold it for a favour seldom known
If he be deigned the honour to sit down.
Soon as the tarts appear: 'Sir Crape, withdraw!
Those dainties are not for a spiritual maw.'
Observe your distance, and be sure to stand
Hard by the cistern with your cap in hand;
There for diversion you may pick your teeth,
Till the kind voider comes for your relief.

90   For mere board-wages such their freedom sell,
Slaves to an hour and vassals to a bell;
And if th'enjoyment of one day be stole,
They are but prisoners out upon parole;
Always the marks of slavery remain,
And they, though loose, still drag about their chain.
    And where's the mighty prospect after all –
A chaplainship served up, and seven years' thrall?
The menial thing perhaps, for a reward,
Is to some slender benefice preferred,

100   With this proviso bound, that he must wed
My Lady's antiquated waiting-maid,
In dressing only skilled, and marmalade.
    Let others, who such meannesses can brook,
Strike countenance to every great man's look;
Let those that have a mind turn slaves to eat,
And live contented by another's plate;
I rate my freedom higher, nor will I
For food and raiment truck my liberty.
But, if I must to my last shifts be put

110   To fill a bladder and twelve yards of gut,
Rather, with counterfeited wooden leg
And my right arm tied up, I'll choose to beg:

I'll rather choose to starve at large than be
The gaudiest vassal to dependency.
   'T has ever been the top of my desires,
The utmost height to which my wish aspires,
That Heav'n would bless me with a small estate,
Where I might find a close, obscure retreat;
There, free from noise and all ambitious ends,
120 Enjoy a few choice books and fewer friends,
Lord of myself, accountable to none
But to my conscience and my God alone;
There live unthought of, and unheard of die,
And grudge mankind my very memory.
But since the blessing is, I find, too great
For me to wish for or expect of Fate,
Yet, maugre all the spite of Destiny,
My thoughts and actions are, and shall be, free.
A certain author, very grave and sage,
130 This story tells (no matter what the page).
   One time, as they walked forth ere break of day,
The Wolf and Dog encountered on the way.
Famished the one, meagre and lean of plight,
As a cast poet who for bread does write;
The other fat and plump as prebend was,
Pampered with luxury and holy ease.
   Thus met, with compliments, too long to tell,
Of being glad to see each well,
'How now, Sir Towzer?' said the Wolf. 'I pray,
140 Whence come it that you look so sleek and gay,
While I, who do as well, I'm sure, deserve,
For want of livelihood am like to starve?'
'Troth, Sir,' replied the Dog, ''t has been my fate,
I thank the friendly stars, to hap of late
On a kind master, to whose care I owe
All this good flesh wherewith you see me now.
From his rich voider every day I'm fed
With bones of fowl and crusts of finest bread,
With fricassee, ragoût, and whatsoe'er
150 Of costly kickshaws now in fashion are,

And more variety of boiled and roast
Than a Lord Mayor's waiter e'er could boast.
Then, Sir, 'tis hardly credible to tell
How I'm respected and beloved by all:
I'm the delight of the whole family,
Not darling Shock more favourite than I.
I never sleep abroad, to air exposed,
But in my warm apartment am inclosed;
There, on fresh bed of straw, with canopy
160   Of hutch above, like dog of state I lie.
Besides, when, with high fare and Nature fired,
To generous sports of youth I am inspired,
All the proud she's are soft to my embrace,
From bitch of quality down to turn-spit race;
Each day I try new mistresses and loves,
Nor envy sovereign dogs in their alcoves.
Thus happy I of all enjoy the best,
No mortal cur on earth yet half so blest:
And, farther to enhance the happiness,
170   All this I get by idleness and ease.'
        'Troth!' said the Wolf. 'I envy your estate.
Would to the gods it were but my good fate
That I might happily admitted be
A member of your blest society!
I would with faithfulness discharge my place
In anything, that I might serve His Grace.
But think you, Sir, it would feasible,
And that my application might prevail?'
        'Do but endeavour, Sir: you need not doubt;
180   I make no question but to bring't about.
Only rely on me, and rest secure.
I'll serve you to the utmost of my power,
As I'm a dog of honour, Sir – but this
I only take the freedom to advise:
That you'd a little lay your roughness by,
And learn to practise complaisance, like me.'
        'For that, let me alone – I'll have a care,
And top my part, I warrant, to a hair;

There's not a courtier of them all shall vie
190 For fawning and for suppleness with me.'
    And thus resolved at last, the travellers
Towards the house together shape their course.
The Dog, who breeding well did understand,
In walking gives his guest the upper hand,
And as they walk along they all the while
With mirth and pleasant raillery beguile
The tedious time and way, till day drew near
And light came on; by which did soon appear
The mastiff's neck to view, all worn and bare.
200   This when his comrade spied: 'What means,' said he,
'This circle bare which round your neck I see?
If I may be so bold—'. 'Sir, you must know
That I at first was rough and fierce, like you;
Of nature curst, and often apt to bite
Strangers, and elsewhoever came in sight.
For this I was tied up, and underwent
The whip sometimes, and such light chastisement,
Till I at length by discipline grew tame,
Gentle, and tractable, as now I am.
210 'Twas by this short and slight severity
I gained these marks and badges which you see.
But what are they? *Allons, Monsieur*! Let's go.'
'Not one step farther, Sir; excuse me now.
Much joy t'ye of your envied, blest estate –
I will not buy preferment at that rate.
    A' God's name, take your golden chains, for me:
    Faith, I'd not be a king, not to be free.
    Sir Dog, your humble servant; so, goodbye.'

The Careless Good Fellow
Written March 9, 1680. Song

A pox of this fooling and plotting of late!
What a pother and stir has it kept in the State?
Let the rabble run mad with suspicions and fears;
Let them scuffle and jar, till they go by the ears;
    Their grievances never shall trouble my pate,
    So I can enjoy my dear bottle at quiet.

What coxcombs were those, who would barter their ease
And their necks for a toy, a thin wafer, and mass?
At old Tyburn they never had needed to swing
10 Had they been but true subjects to drink and their King;
    A friend and a bottle is all my design;
    He has no room for treason that's top-full of wine.

I mind not the Members, and makers of laws:
Let them sit or prorogue, as His Majesty please;
Let them damn us to woollen, I'll never repine
At my lodging when dead, so alive I have wine;
    Yet oft, in my drink, I can hardly forbear
    To curse them for making my claret so dear.

I mind not grave asses, who idly debate
20 About Right and Succession, the trifles of state;
We've a good King already, and he deserves laughter
That will trouble his head with who shall come after;
    Come, here's to his health, and I wish he may be
    As free from all care and all trouble as we.

What care I how leagues with the Hollander go,
Or intrigues betwixt Sidney and Monsieur D'Avaux?
What concerns it my drinking if Cassel be sold,
If the conqueror take it by storming or gold?
    Good Bordeaux alone is the place that I mind,
30   And when the fleet's coming, I pray for a wind.

The Bully of France, that aspires to renown
By dull cutting of throats, and venturing his own:
Let him fight and be damned, and make matches, and treat,
To afford the news-mongers and coffee-house, chat;
    He's but a brave wretch, while I am more free,
    More safe, and a thousand times happier than he.

Come he, or the Pope, or the Devil to boot,
Or come faggot and stake: I care not a groat.
Never think that in Smithfield I porters will heat;
40   No, I swear, Mr Foxe: pray excuse me for that.
    I'll drink, in defiance of gibbet and halter;
    This is the profession that never will alter.

A Satire
*The Person of Spenser is brought in, Dissuading the Author
from the Study of Poetry and Showing how Little it is
Esteemed and Encouraged in this Present Age*

One night, as I was pondering of late
On all the miseries of my hapless fate,
Cursing my rhyming stars, raving in vain
At all the powers which over poets reign:
In came a ghastly Shape, all pale and thin,
As some poor sinner who by priest had been
Under a long Lent's penance starved and whipped,
Or parboiled lecher, late from hothouse crept.
Famished his looks appeared, his eyes sunk in;
10   Like morning-gown about him hung his skin;
A wreath of laurel on his head he wore;
A book, inscribed *The Faerie Queene*, he bore.
    By this I knew him, rose and bowed, and said:
'Hail, reverend Ghost! All hail, most sacred Shade!
Why this great visit? Why vouchsafed to me,
The meanest of thy British progeny?
Com'st thou in my uncalled, unhallowed Muse
Some of thy mighty spirit to infuse?

If so, lay on thy hands, ordain me fit
20   For the high cure and ministry of Wit;
Let me, I beg, thy great instructions claim;
Teach me to tread the glorious paths of Fame.
Teach me (for none does better know than thou)
How, like thyself, I may immortal grow.'
      Thus did I speak, and spoke it in a strain
Above my common rate and usual vein,
As if inspired by presence of the Bard,
Who, with a frown, thus to reply was heard,
In style of satire, such wherein of old
30   He the famed tale of *Mother Hubberd* told.
      'I come, fond idiot, ere it be too late,
Kindly to warn thee of thy wretched fate.
Take heed betimes, repent, and learn of me
To shun the dangerous rocks of Poetry.
Had I the choice of flesh and blood again,
To act once more in life's tumultous scene,
I'd be a porter, or a scavenger,
A groom, or anything but poet here.
Hast thou observed some hawker of the town,
40   Who through the streets, with dismal scream and tone,
Cries "Matches, small coal, brooms, old shoes and boots,
Socks, sermons, ballads, lies, gazettes, and votes"?
So unrecorded to the grave I'd go,
And nothing but the register tell, who;
Rather that poor, unheard-of wretch I'd be,
Than the most glorious name in poetry,
With all its boasted immortality.
Rather than he who sang, on Phrygia's shore,
The Grecian bullies fighting for a whore;
50   Or he of Thebes, whom fame so much extols
For praising jockeys and Newmarket fools.
      'So many, now, and bad the scribblers be,
'Tis scandal to be of the company;
The foul disease is so prevailing grown,
So much the fashion of the Court and Town,
That scarce a man well bred in either's deemed

But who has killed, been often clapped, and oft has
    rhymed.
The fools are troubled with a flux of brains,
And each on paper squirts his filthy sense;
60   A leash of sonnets and a dull lampoon
Set up an author, who forthwith is grown
A man of parts, of rhyming, and renown.
Ev'n that vile wretch who, in lewd verse, each year
Describes the pageants and my good Lord Mayor –
Whose works must serve, the next election-day,
For making squibs, and under pies to lay –
Yet counts himself of the inspirèd train,
And dares in thought the sacred name profane.
  '"But is it nought," thou'lt say, "in front to stand,
70   With laurel crowned, by White or Loggan's hand?
Is it not great and glorious to be known,
Marked out, and gazed at through the wondering town,
By all the rabble passing up and down?"
So Oats and Bedloe have been pointed at,
And every busy coxcomb of the State;
The meanest felons who through Holborn go,
More eyes and looks than twenty poets draw.
If this be all, go, have thy posted name
Fixed up with bills of quack and public shame;
80   To be the stop of gaping prentices,
And read by reeling drunkards when they piss;
Or else to lie exposed on trading stall,
While the bilked owner hires gazettes, to tell
('Mongst "Spaniels Lost") that "Author Does Not Sell".
  'Perhaps, fond fools, thou sooth'st thyself in dream
With hopes of purchasing a lasting name?
Thou think'st, perhaps, thy trifles shall remain,
Like sacred Cowley and immortal Ben?
But who, of all the bold adventurers
90   Who now drive on the trade of fame in verse,
Can be ensured, in this unfaithful sea
Where there so many lost and shipwrecked be?
How many poems writ in ancient time,
Which thy forefathers had in great esteem,

Which in the crowded shops bore any rate,
And sold like news-books and affairs of state,
Have grown contemptible and slighted since,
As Pordage, Flecknoe, or the *British Prince*?
Quarles, Chapman, Heywood, Withers had applause,
100   And Wild, and Ogilby, in former days,
But now are damned to wrapping drugs and wares,
And cursed by all their broken stationers;
And so may'st thou, perchance, pass up and down,
And please a while th'admiring Court and Town,
Who after shalt in Duck Lane shops be thrown,
To mould with Sylvester and Shirley there,
And truck for pots of ale next Stourbridge Fair.
Then who'll not laugh, to see th'immortal name
To vile mundungus made a martyr-flame,
110   And all thy deathless monuments of Wit
Wipe porters' tails or mount in paper kite?
     'But grant thy poetry should find success,
And (which is rare) the squeamish critics please;
Admit it read and praised and courted be
By this nice age and all posterity:
If thou expectest ought but empty Fame,
Condemn thy hopes and labours to the flame.
The rich have now learned only to admire;
He who to greater favours does aspire
120   Is mercenary thought and writes to hire.
Wouldst thou, to raise thine and thy country's fame,
Choose some old English hero for thy theme:
Bold Arthur, or great Edward's greater son,
Or our fifth Harry, matchless in renown;
Make Agincourt and Cressy fields outvie
The famed Lavinian shores and walls of Troy;
What Scipio, what Maecenas wouldst thou find,
What Sidney now, to thy great project kind?
"Bless me! How great genius! How each line
130   Is big with sense! How glorious a design
Does through the whole and each proportion shine!
How lofty all his thoughts, and how inspired!
Pity such wondrous parts are not preferred" –

Cries a gay, wealthy sot, who would not bail
For bare five pounds the author out of jail
Should he starve there and rot; who, if a brief
Came out the needy poets to relieve,
To the whole tribe would scarce a tester give,
But fifty guineas for a whore and clap!
140 The peer's well used, and comes off wondrous cheap;
A poet would be dear and out o'th'way
Should he expect above a coach-man's pay.
For this will any dedicate and lie,
And daub the gaudy ass with flattery?
For this will any prostitute his sense
To coxcombs, void of bounty as of brains?
Yet such is the hard fate of writers now,
They're forced for alms to each great name to bow;
Fawn like her lap-dog on Her tawdry Grace,
150 Commend her beauty and belie her glass
(By which she every morning primes her face);
Sneak to His Honour, call him witty, brave,
And just, though a known coward, fool, or knave;
And praise his lineage and nobility,
Whose arms at first came from the Company.
 ''Tis so, 'twas ever so, since heretofore
The blind old Bard, with dog and bell before,
Was fain to sing for bread from door to door;
The needy Muses all turned gipsies then,
160 And of the begging trade e'er since have been.
Should mighty Sappho in these days revive
And hope upon her stock of wit to live,
She must to Cresswell's trudge to mend her gains,
And let her tail to hire, as well as brains.
What poet ever fined for sheriff? Or who
By wit and sense did ever Lord Mayors grow?
 'My own hard usage here I need not press,
Where you have every day before your face
Plenty of fresh, resembling instances.
170 Great Cowley's Muse the same ill treatment had,
Whose verse shall live for ever, to upbraid
Th'ingrateful world, that left such worth unpaid.

Waller himself may thank inheritance
For what he else had never got by sense.
On Butler who can think without just rage,
The glory and the scandal of the age?
Fair stood his hopes when first he came to town:
Met everywhere with welcomes of renown,
Courted and loved by all, with wonder read,
180 And promises of princely favour, fed.
But what reward for all had he at last,
After a life in dull expectance passed?
The wretch, at summing up his misspent days,
Found nothing left but poverty and praise;
Of all his gains by verse, he could not save
Enough to purchase flannel and a grave;
Reduced to want, he in due time fell sick,
Was fain to die and be interred on tick,
And well might bless the fever, that was sent
190 To rid him hence and his worse fate prevent.
      'You've seen what fortune other poets share;
View next the factors of the theatre:
That constant mart which all the year does hold,
Where staple wit is bartered, bought, and sold;
Here trading scribblers, for their maintainance
And livelihood, trust to a lottery chance.
But who his parts would in the service spend
Where all his hopes on vulgar breath depend?
Where every sot, for paying half a crown,
200 Has the prerogative to cry him down?
Sedley indeed may be content with fame,
Nor care should an ill-judging audience damn;
But Settle, and the rest that write for pence,
Whose whole estate's an ounce or two of brains,
Should a thin house on the third day appear,
Must starve, or live in tatters all the year.
And what can we expect that's brave and great,
From a poor, needy wretch, that writes to eat?
Who the success of the next play must wait
210 For lodging, food, and clothes, and whose chief care
Is how to sponge for the next meal, and where?

'Hadst thou of old in flourishing Athens lived,
When all the learned arts in glory thrived,
When mighty Sophocles the stage did sway,
And poets by the State were held in pay,
'Twere worth thy pains to cultivate thy Muse,
And daily wonders then it might produce;
But who would now write hackney to a stage
That's only thought the nuisance of the age?
220 Go, after this, and beat thy wretched brains,
And toil to bring in thankless idiots' means;
Turn o'er dull Horace and the Classic fools,
To poach for sense and hunt for idle rules;
Be free of tickets and the play-houses,
To make some tawdry actress there thy prize,
And spend thy third day's gains 'twixt her clapped thighs.
'All trades and all professions here abound,
And yet encouragement for all is found;
Here, a vile emp'ric (who by licence kills,
230 Who every week helps to increase the bills)
Wears velvet, keeps his coach and whore beside,
For what less villains must to Tyburn ride.
There, a dull, trading sot, in wealth o'ergrown
By thriving knavery, can call his own
A dozen manors, and, if Fate still bless,
Expects as many counties to possess.
Punks, panders, bawds, all their due pensions gain,
And every day the great men's bounty drain;
Lavish expence on wit has never yet
240 Been taxed amongst the grievances of state.
The Turkey, Guinea, India, gainers be,
And all, but the Poetic Company;
Each place of traffic – Bantam, Smyrna, Zante,
Greenland, Virginia, Seville, Alicante,
And France, that sends us dildoes, lace, and wine –
Vast profit all and large returns bring in;
Parnassus only is that barren coast
Where the whole voyage and adventure's lost.
'Then be advised: the slighted Muse forsake,
250 And Coke and Dalton for thy study take;

For fees each term, sweat in the crowded hall,
And there for charters and cracked titles bawl:
Where Maynard thrives, and pockets more each year
Than forty laureates of the theatre.
Or else to orders and the Church betake
Thyself, and that thy future refuge make;
There fawn on some proud patron, to engage
Th'advowson of cast punk and parsonage;
Or soothe the Court and preach up kingly Right,
260   To gain a prebendery and mitre by't.
In fine: turn pettifogger, canonist,
Civilian, pedant, mountebank, or priest,
Soldier, or merchant, fiddler, painter, fencer,
Jack-pudding, juggler, player, or rope-dancer;
Preach, plead, cure, fight, game, pimp, beg, cheat, or
        thieve;
Be all but poet, and there's way to live.
    'But why do I in vain my counsel spend
On one whom there's so little hope to mend,
Where I perhaps as fruitlessly exhort
270   As Lenten doctors when they preach at Court?
Not entered punks from lust they once have tried,
Not fops and women from conceit and pride,
Not bawds from impudence, cowards from fear,
Nor seared, unfeeling sinners past despair,
Are half so hard and stubborn to reduce
As a poor wretch, when once possessed with Muse.
    'If, therefore, what I've said cannot avail,
Nor from the rhyming folly thee recall,
But, spite of all, thou wilt be obstinate
280   And run thyself upon avoidless Fate:
May'st thou go on, unpitied, till thou be
Brought to the parish, bridge, and beggary;
Till, urged by want, like broken scribblers, thou
Turn poet to a booth, a Smithfield show,
And write heroic verse for Barthol'mew.
    'Then, slighted by the very Nursery,
    May'st thou at last be forced to starve, like me.'

from *The Thirteenth Satire of Juvenal, Imitated*

Little do folks the Heav'nly Powers mind,
If they but 'scape the knowledge of mankind.
Observe, with how demure and grave a look
The rascal lays his hand upon the Book;
Then, with a praying face and lifted eye,
Claps on his lips and seals the perjury.
If you persist his innocence to doubt
And boggle in belief, he'll straight rap out
Oaths by the volley, each of which would make
10 Pale atheists start and trembling bullies quake,
And more than would a whole ship's crew maintain
To the East Indies hence and back again.
'As God shall pardon me, Sir, I am free
Of what you charge me with; let me ne'er see
His face in Heaven else; may these hands rot,
These eyes drop out, if I e'er had a groat
Of yours, or if they ever touched or saw't.'
Thus he'll run on, two hours in length, till he
Spin out a curse long as the Litany;
20 Till Heav'n has scarce a judgment left in store
For him to wish, deserve, or suffer more.
    There are who disavow all Providence,
And think the world is only steered by Chance;
Make God at best an idle looker-on,
A lazy monarch lolling in his throne,
Who his affairs does neither mind or know,
But leaves them all at random here below;
And such at every foot themselves will damn,
And oaths no more than common breath esteem.
30 No shame nor loss of ears can frighten these,
Were every street a grove of pillories.
    Others there be that own a God, and fear
His vengeance to ensue, and yet forswear.
Thus to himself says one, 'Let Heav'n decree
What doom soe'er its pleasure will of me:

Strike me with blindness, palsies, leprosies,
Plague, pox, consumption, all the maladies
Of both the 'spitals; so I get my prize
And hold it sure, I'll suffer these, and more;
40 All plagues are light to that of being poor.'
There's not a begging cripple in the streets
(Unless he with his limbs has lost his wits,
And is grown fit for Bedlam) but, no doubt,
To have his wealth would have the rich man's gout.
'Grant Heaven's vengeance heavy be; what though?
The heaviest things move slowliest still, we know:
And, if it punish all that guilty be,
'Twill be an age before it come to me.
God too is merciful as well as just,
50 Therefore I'll rather his forgiveness trust
Than live despised and poor, as thus I must.
I'll try, and hope he's more a gentleman
Than for such trivial things as these to damn.
Besides, for the same fact we've often known
One mount the cart, another mount the throne;
And foulest deeds, attended with success,
No longer are reputed wickedness,
Disguised with Virtue's livery and dress.'
     With these weak arguments, they fortify
60 And harden up themselves in villainy.
The rascal now dares call you to account,
And in what court you please join issue on't;
Next term he'll bring the action to be tried,
And twenty witnesses to swear on's side,
And, if that justice to his cause be found,
Expects a verdict of five hundred pound.
Thus he, who boldly dares the guilt outface,
For innocent shall with the rabble pass;
While you, with impudence and sham run down,
70 Are only thought the knave by all the town.

For an Anniversary of Music kept upon
St Cecilia's Day

Begin the song! Your instruments advance!
   Tune the voice and tune the flute;
   Touch the silent, sleeping lute,
And make the strings to their own measures dance.
Bring gentlest thoughts that into language glide,
Bring softest words that into numbers slide;
   Let every hand, let every tongue,
   To make the noble consort, throng;
Let all in one harmonious note agree
10   To frame the mighty song,
For this is Music's sacred jubilee.

Hark! How the wakened strings resound,
   And sweetly break the yielding air!
The ravished sense how pleasingly they wound,
   And call the listening soul into the ear!
Each pulse beats time, and every heart
With tongue and fingers bears a part.
   By Harmony's entrancing power
When we are thus wound up to ecstasy,
20   Methinks we mount, methinks we tower,
     And seem to leave mortality,
And seem to antedate our future bliss on high!

How dull were life, how hardly worth our care,
   But for the charms which Music lends!
How palled its pleasures would appear,
   But for the pleasure which our art attends!
    Without the sweets of melody
     To tune our vital breath,
    Who would not give it up to death,
30   And in the silent grave contented lie?

Music's the cordial of a troubled breast,
    The softest remedy that grief can find;
The gentle spell that charms our cares to rest,
    And calms the ruffling passions of the mind.
    Music does all our joys refine,
    'Tis that gives relish to our wine,
        'Tis that gives rapture to our love;
    It wings devotion to a pitch divine,
'Tis our chief bliss on earth and half our Heav'n above.

Chorus

40   Come then with tuneful breath and string;
        The praises of our art let's sing;
        Let's sing to blest Cecilia's fame,
    That graced this art and gave this day its name;
        While music, wine, and mirth conspire
        To bear a consort and make up the choir.

NOTES

Critical works cited below that appear in Further Reading are here referred to by author/editor surname and short title.

ABRAHAM COWLEY

The following abbreviations have been used for the texts on which these poems have been based. In every case but two the text is the last published in Cowley's lifetime or the first published after it: the exceptions are the extract from *The Civil War*, which is taken from the 1989 volume of *The Collected Works* instead of the first publication of it by Pritchard in 1973, and the 'Sors Virgiliana', which is taken from a manuscript copy by John Aubrey.

MS: British Library, London, Lansdowne MS 231
Poetical: *Poetical Blossoms* (1636) (second edition)
Poems: *Poems* (1656)
Verses: *Verses Written upon Several Occasions* (1663)
Works: Thomas Sprat (ed.), *The Works of Mr Abraham Cowley* (1668)
Poemata: Thomas Sprat (ed.), *Poemata Latina* (1668)
Collected Works: Thomas O. Calhoun, Laurence Heyworth, et al. (eds.),
      The Collected Works of Abraham Cowley (1989–)

A Vote

Poetical. Written, according to Cowley, at the age of thirteen, 'A Vote' (that is, a prayer) anticipates the classical themes of modest contentment and retirement that he would develop in his late verse and *Essays*. He used these final stanzas again, on their own, in his essay 'Of Myself', remarking, with apparent surprise: 'The beginning of [the poem] is boyish, but of this part . . . (if a very little were corrected) I should hardly now be much ashamed.' He made only two significant verbal 'corrections': 'unknown' for the less usual 'ignote' (line 5), and 'have' for the warmer 'hug' (line 7).

Against Fruition

Poems; first published in 1647. For the subject of this poem, see note to Waller, 'In Answer of Sir John Suckling's Verses'. Cowley gives it unusual piquancy by making the speaker address the woman, producing an anti-seduction poem.

Cowley's argument depends not, like the 'Petronius' fragment, on the nausea induced by sex, but on the importance of mystery – backed with a provocative religious analogy. The satiated lover will be like Alexander the Great (born at Pella, in Macedon), who was said to have wept at having no more worlds to conquer (lines 13–14). 'Admire' (lines 25–6) is a significant pun: the original meaning is 'wonder at'. The poem ends with Cupid, the winged god of love: Cowley imagines him first like a hawk, finally like a bee.

The Heart-Breaking

Poems; first published in 1647. In this poem, love begins as poison, which cracks fine glass (an idea found elsewhere in literature of this period: see, for example, Donne, 'Elegy on the Lady Markham' (1609), line 42). Poison suggests snakes. Snakes can survive if cut to pieces (in line 12, 'which' is the subject, 'the whole' the object of 'kill'). Division suggests anarchy. The final image strangely anticipates the events of 1649–60, as seen by Cowley: in his ode on the Restoration, the multiplying serpent is an image for Oliver Cromwell.

The Motto

Poems. This poem appeared first at the end of *The Mistress* (1647), where it was presented by the publisher as a substitute for a frontispiece: 'being ... (as I conceive) the more lively representation of him'. The Latin epigraph is a quotation from Virgil, Georgics III. 8–9: 'A way must be tried by which I too can lift myself from the earth and fly victorious over the lips of men.'

Dr Johnson recommended this poem, but thought it should be called 'To my Muse' – the addressee of the second couplet. Cowley, lacking the advantages of great birth, is the flint of fortune who will produce fire only if he is struck ('strook': line 12); he aspires to poetic immortality, which he describes as the trumpet which at Last Judgment will summon bodies from their graves (lines 15–16). He then pits himself against heroes of antiquity, beginning with the least literary and ending with the most. Hannibal, the great Carthaginian general, marched across the Alps in his campaign against Rome in 218 BC (lines 17–18). Aristotle, born in Stagyra, was the tutor of

Alexander the Great: the great philosopher made himself master of far
more than the great commander, says Cowley (lines 27–30). Cicero was a
Roman statesman, but it is his great oratory that continues to preserve
Rome's reputation (lines 31–4). Virgil, born in Mantua, is a 'Swan' because
he 'sings', that is, writes poetry (lines 35–8). 'Rage' in line 38 is poetic
frenzy; the contrast is presumably between him and Homer, whose work
is less verbally artful – a comparison that was to become commonplace later
in the century (see in particular the Prefaces to Dryden's translation of the
Aeneid (1697) and to his *Fables* (1700)).

On the Death of Sir Anthony Van Dyck

Poems. For the subject of this poem, see note to Waller, 'To Van Dyck'.
The painter died in 1641.
  Cowley begins by marking a parallel between painting and poetry: both
have Muses, and Van Dyck's death turns the second as mute as the first
(lines 1–4). Comparison between the two was a favourite theme for critics,
usually inspired by Horace's dictum in the *Ars Poetica*: 'Poetry is like
painting.' (For an influential development of the comparison later in the
century, see Waller, 'Instructions to a Painter'.) Van Dyck's paintings
are praised here for their naturalism: they are more like their subjects
than twins are like each other (lines 11–14). The word 'colour' in line
19 is a pun: it has also the meaning 'pretence', thus summing up the
shift from aesthetic to moral praise. Van Dyck is now in Heaven, where he
is welcomed by St Luke, the patron saint of painters, and sees the ideas in
the mind of God which, according to a Platonic tradition of thought, are
the originals of things on earth. The elegy ends in a conventional manner,
with praise and consolation for the widow; the 'new-born you' of line 40
refers to their daughter, Justiniana, born eight days before the painter's
death.

THE CIVIL WAR

Book II [The Devil Speaks]

Collected Works. The first five hundred lines of Book I of this poem were
first published after Cowley's death, in 1679; the rest of it (another two
books) were edited by Allan Pritchard in 1973. The poem covers the events
of the war down to the Battle of Newbury (September 1643) from a
relentlessly partisan perspective. Immediately before the present passage,
the Royalists have captured Bristol and Exeter, and begun to lay siege to
Gloucester, at present in Parliament's hands; Hell, which backs Parliament,

is disturbed at the way things are going. For a full commentary, see *Collected Works*, I, and Pritchard, *The Civil War*.

The parliamentary leaders listed by Belzebub are Nathaniel Fiennes (line 23), who surrendered Bristol to Prince Rupert; his father, Viscount Saye and Sele; John Pym (both line 34); Oliver St John, the Solicitor-General, and his cousin, the Earl of Bolingbroke; the two Sir Henry Vanes, father and son; and the Earl of Manchester (Lord Kimbolton was one of his titles) (all line 42). Saye and Bolingbroke were parliamentary champions in the House of Lords; Pym, St John and the Vanes champions in the Commons; Manchester was at this time one of Parliament's chief military leaders. 'Lud's seditious town' (line 35) is London, seat of Parliament, now abandoned by the King (who had set up a Parliament of his own at Oxford) and considered by Royalists a centre of sedition. The innovations approved by the Devil include the abolition of the office of bishop, claimed by Anglicans to be of enormous antiquity (lines 29–30), and the sequestering of the Church's lands (lines 71–3). By contrast, the Puritan preachers are doing the devil's work: Cowley accuses them, in traditional style, of venality, disloyalty and fake spirituality (lines 85 ff.: 'their islands and New World' (line 90) is a reference to the Puritan colonial ventures in Providence Island, lost to the Spaniards in 1641; Puritan claims of direct inspiration from God were regarded with hatred by their enemies). To express the scale of the horror, Cowley draws on Roman history and on the Bible. Catiline was a Roman revolutionary leader, defeated by the actions of Cicero (lines 56–8); Marius and Sulla were earlier revolutionaries, infamous in particular for the proscriptions by which they marked down their enemies for death (line 80). The 'voice' (line 39) heard as God left Jerusalem is a reference apparently to Ezekiel 1:24–5; for the plagues of Egypt (line 98) (on which Cowley had written a Pindaric Ode), see Exodus 7–12.

[Sors Virgiliana]

MS. First published by Charles Gildon in *Miscellany Poems* (1692); the present text comes from the manuscript copy by John Aubrey. According to the commonest version of the much-told story, Charles I, in the early years of the Civil War, insisted on trying the 'sortes Virgilianae' ('Virgilian lots') – the old custom of picking a passage of the *Aeneid* at random, to learn one's future. The book opened at Dido's curse on Aeneas at the end of Book IV. Cowley was asked to translate the fortune into verse, without being told whose it was. In a letter to Henry Bennet in April 1650, the year after the King's death, Cowley writes that he is encouraged about affairs in Scotland because 'Virgil has told me something . . .' (T. Brown (ed.), *Miscellanea Aulica* . . . (London, 1702) p. 130).

On the Death of Mr Crashaw

Poems. Richard Crashaw (1612/13–49), poet and mystic, had been a friend of Cowley at Cambridge; he left in early 1644, as the Puritans were taking control of the university and beginning to 'reform' the colleges; at around this time, he converted to Catholicism. In 1645, he met Cowley again in the exiles' court in France, and was introduced by him to the Catholic Queen, Henrietta Maria, through whose influence he obtained a succession of Church posts in Italy. He died, perhaps of fever, in Loretto.

In the first three words of the poem, Cowley sets the terms of his praise for Crashaw. The poem uses biblical and classical images, in stark opposition. Crashaw is compared first to Moses, who led the Israelites out of Egypt (hence away from 'Pyramids'), just as the poet led the Muses to their proper destination: praise of God (lines 5–8). Among Crashaw's contemporaries, meanwhile, poetry ('numbers'), potentially 'heavenly', 'keeps up Hell' by celebrating pagan gods (lines 17–18). According to a legend reported by Plutarch, a voice was heard at the time of the Crucifixion, crying that Pan (a classical woodland god) was dead. Apollo, believed by the Greeks to speak through oracles, survives in that he is the god of paganizing poetry (lines 21–2). 'Calves at Bethel' (line 20), made of gold, were set up by the renegade King Jeroboam as objects for idolatrous worship (I Kings 12:28–30). From idolatry, Cowley moves to love-poetry. Poets idolize women, although the first woman was responsible for the loss of Paradise: women's eyes are compared in this sort of poetry to 'stars', thought responsible for human 'fate' by those with astrological beliefs, and the poets combine the female faults of looseness and story-telling (being 'fabulous') (lines 23–8). Crashaw's Muse, by contrast, was devoted to, and is here partially equated with, the Virgin Mary (lines 29–30: 'but' in line 34 means 'anyone except') – object of much greater reverence among Catholics than Protestants. She was worshipped at the shrine in Loretto, which was supposed to have been her original home, transported to the site from the Holy Land by a miracle (lines 39–44). Cowley offers a remarkably generous tribute to the apostate's spirituality, ending with a vow to ask Crashaw to intercede with God on his behalf, as Catholics (but not Protestants) asked saints. 'Nice tenets' (line 55) are pedantic points of doctrine, contrasted with Crashaw's virtuous life. In Heaven, Crashaw becomes a 'Bard Triumphant' (line 59) – phraseology adapted from the Church Militant and the Church Triumphant: the body of the faithful on earth, and those in Heaven. The poem ends with the two poets united in another Old Testament simile: the prophet Elijah was taken up to Heaven in a chariot of fire; his mantle descended on the prophet Elisha, who had requested it, along with twice Elijah's 'spirit' (line 71), or gift of prophecy (2 Kings 2:9–13).

ANACREONTICS

Poems. The *Anacreontea* are sixty-one short poems on love, wine and the good life, believed until the eighteenth century to be by the Greek lyric poet Anacreon (*c.*575–490 BC), now thought to be much later; in 1554, Henri Estienne produced an edition, with Latin translation, of fifty-five of them, which became highly popular. Cowley translated eleven, which have always been among the best loved of his poems. For an attractive introduction to them, see Tom Mason, 'Cowley and the Wisdom of Anacreon', *Cambridge Quarterly* 19 (1990), 103–37. Cowley's contemporary Thomas Stanley translated all fifty-five: his approach is much less adventurous.

II Drinking

A rollicking expansion of the brief Greek original. Compare Oldham, 'An Ode of Anacreon Paraphrased: The Cup' – a version of another 'anacreontic'. A 'health' (line 16) is a toast.

V Age

The image in the last line is drawn from gambling.

X The Grasshopper

Cowley's Grasshopper is a true follower of the Greek philosopher Epicurus, who taught that the good life is that devoted to simple pleasure. In his *Essays*, Cowley explores the Epicurean philosophy at length. He was aware also, however, of the popular conception of Epicureanism, as a self-indulgent creed of excess: another of his 'Epicurean animals', the City Mouse, seems to exemplify this (see note to 'The Country Mouse'). In its ideal existence, the Grasshopper is surrounded by its own kinds of deity: it receives moisture as if from Ganymede, cupbearer to the gods (Cowley uses a variant form of his name in line 8 for the rhyme); Phoebus Apollo, as god of the sun and of music, is its father (line 24).

Brutus

Poems. Marcus Junius Brutus joined the conspiracy to assassinate Julius Caesar in 44 BC; defeated at Philippi in 31 BC by Mark Antony and Octavian (later Augustus), he killed himself. Compare the treatment of this span of

Roman history in Waller, 'A Panegyric to my Lord Protector'. According to a later tradition, Cowley's praise of the Republican hero cost him the favour of the King. Recent critics have argued that the poem is in fact anti-Cromwellian: Caesar is not the King, but the current ruler, as Cromwell was; Cowley associates Cromwell elsewhere with Octavian and Antony, Brutus's enemies; and the reward for patience promised in the last stanza is to see the true King (the parallel is hardly blasphemous by the standards of some Royalist writing). Psychologically, however, the poem looks more complex: the clear echo of *Hamlet* in the fourth stanza suggests a deeply ambiguous attitude to Brutus, who was widely rumoured to be Caesar's son.

Brutus was praised in antiquity for his extraordinary moral integrity; Cowley starts with a Platonic picture whereby the blindness of the majority to the 'idea' or true essence of Virtue prevents appreciation of Brutus's qualities (lines 23–7). Caesar's attack on Rome is seen as an act of sexual violence, worse than his successor Nero's matricide ((lines 32–42: 'parricide' in older English can apply to both parents): the implicit connexion between them is incest, as Caesar was said to have dreamed, before his crucial step of crossing the river Rubicon, that he was making love to his mother, and Nero was said to have been his mother's lover. By contrast with Caesar, Brutus refused (or would have refused) supreme power even when offered it (lines 43–6). This offer, not in the ancient sources, was probably taken from Shakespeare, *Julius Caesar*, III. ii; in the fourth stanza the visit of the unnamed, revenging ghost to Brutus (described by Plutarch) is conflated with the appearance of the dead king at the beginning of *Hamlet* (compare the cock-crow (line 55) and the dawn moving up the 'eastern hill' (line 57)). The last stanza picks up the hint of line 2: the pagan ideal of a steady and self-sufficient virtue is 'confounded' (line 85) by the Christian ideal of God's free grace to fallen man.

To Mr Hobbes

Poems. Thomas Hobbes (1588–1679), the best-known and most controversial English political philosopher of the seventeenth century, was, like Cowley, attached to the exiled court in Paris in the 1640s. *Leviathan* (1651), in which he advocates obedience even to a usurping ruler, caused a scandal among Royalists, rather like Cowley's encomium of Brutus (see 'Brutus'). The poem is a Pindaric Ode – an irregular form made very popular by Cowley; Cowley provided his own notes for his odes, which are quoted below.

The organic coherence of Hobbes's philosophy is given a physical analogy in the first stanza: like nature, it detests a vacuum ('emptiness') (line 16). The great rival in the second stanza is Aristotle, 'the mighty Stagyrite' (line 17) (see 'The Motto'). Cowley's notes explain the 'leopard' and the 'eagle' (lines 19–20): the Aristotelian philosophy 'Outlasted the Graecian Empire, which, in the Visions of Daniel, is represented by a leopard, with four wings upon the back, and four heads'; it was 'received even beyond the bounds of the Roman Empire, and outlived it', achieving particular importance among the Arabs despite the anti-intellectualist teaching of Mahomet (born in Mecca: line 22). A 'deluge' (line 23) of invaders from 'the Turks, and other nations' drove it west, where it provided a basis for the Medieval scholastic philosophers, and was killed off by their pedantry (a facile commonplace). Hobbes's much-needed originality is expressed in the third stanza by the image of exhausted ground, where even food is now wanting, although lesser contemporaries still try vainly to detect precious metal with hazel branches ('divining wands': line 44). The Euxine (line 49) is the Black Sea; the seas are another image for old knowledge, for 'all the navigation of the ancients was in these seas' (Cowley's note). In the fifth stanza, Cowley marvels that there are words in which to dress out 'his notions . . . so new, and so great'; Hobbes's reasoning is compared to the shield made for the Trojan hero Aeneas by the blacksmith god, Vulcan, which shattered swords that tried to pierce it – 'just the case of men's arguing against solid, and that is, divine Reason' (Cowley's note). In the final stanza, Hobbes, white-haired but intellectually vigorous, is compared to the volcano Etna, covered in snow but full of flame – an image derived from the *Anacreontea*. Hobbes had protested with spirit against despising the old at the end of his exchange with Davenant, published with Cowley's and Waller's commendatory poems in the 1650 edition of *Gondibert*.

The Muse

Poems. A declaration of belief in the power of poetry. The poem makes a striking contrast with Waller, 'Upon the Earl of Roscommon's Translation . . .'; Cowley too, however, is careful to include poetic technicalities in the Muse's train, and to pair Fancy with Judgment.

Cowley imagines in the first stanza a carriage with six horses: Fancy, Judgment, Wit, Eloquence, Memory, and Invention (creativeness), 'traced' or harnessed together; Nature controls the first pair of horses, Art the second and third (lines 3–9). Running along beside it are the footmen: figures of speech, ingenious images, ecstatic outpourings and epigrams. They must hurry up ('put on': line 17) because man's life is short, like a day in winter. In the second stanza, they cross the sea, described in terms of air, and air, described in terms of sea. In the third stanza, the Muse plumbs the depths of time, and looks at the unborn years through their amniotic sac ('secondine': line 50). In the last stanza, movement stops, as she preserves the present moment in a sweet substance (probably honey), solidifies it, and extends it: Cowley's note explains that 'There are two sorts of eternity: from the present backwards to eternity, and from the present forwards . . . These two make up the whole circle of eternity, which the present time cuts like a diameter, but poetry makes it extend to all eternity to come, which is the half-circle.'

DAVIDEIS

Book I [Music]

Poems. This passage occurs half-way through Book I: Saul has summoned David, noted for his musical skill, to play for him. Cowley's note gives the origin of the passage as 1 Samuel 16:23, though he has moved it to a point where Saul is already angry, and expanded it into something new.

Cowley's praise of music, which is also a praise of poetry ('numbers': line 2), goes beyond sound (no more than an outward manifestation or 'dressing': line 26) to the principles of harmony: the artist is 'godlike' (line 8) in his power to create and to order. Underlying the analogy is the ancient idea of the music of the spheres – cosmic music produced by the heavenly bodies in their regular movement (see also note to Waller, 'Song ("Behold the brand of Beauty tossed")')'; related to the analogy is the equally ancient idea, to which Cowley refers, of man as a microcosm, or 'lesser' (line 30) world. The 'sympathy' (line 34: literally, the shared feeling) between micro- and macrocosm means that music does not need force to make its effect: it has a 'party' (line 36) or faction acting for it within the listener. The analogy is illustrated by the vibration of a string when an adjacent one is touched, and by the belief that a wound could be cured by applying a healing salve to the spilt blood (Cowley's contemporary Sir Kenelm Digby, to whom he dedicated an early work, patented a 'sympathetic powder' which was supposed to work something like this). With the 'unformed hint' of line 7, compare Oldham, 'A Letter from the Country to a Friend in Town', lines 162 ff.

Book III [Lot's Wife]

Cowley's excuse for this extraordinary piece of description is a picture of the story of Lot seen by David in the King of Moab's palace. Warned by God, Lot fled from the wicked city of Sodom just before it was burned down; his wife could not resist looking back, and was turned into a 'pillar of salt' (Genesis19:26). In a note on this passage, Cowley considers and dismisses the idea that the phrase must be taken metaphorically. A modern poem which achieves a slightly similar effect is Wallace Stevens, 'The Worms at Heaven's Gate'.

On the Queen's Repairing Somerset House

Works. 1668. For the subject, see Waller, 'Upon Her Majesty's New Buildings at Somerset House'. This poem was entered in the Stationers' Register together with Waller's poem in November 1664; an elegy for Cowley, published 1667, refers to it, which suggests that it was published before 1668, but no copy seems to have survived. Written in the person of Somerset House, it offers a grand panorama of London, displaying on a smaller scale the technique of symbolic topography made famous by Sir John Denham in *Cooper's Hill* (first published in 1642). Denham was writing at the beginning of the Civil War, and his landscape is enriched by a sense of anxiety and conflict; Cowley, writing after the Restoration, offers a less demanding vision. (For further commentary, see Fowler, *Country House Poem*, pp. 342–3.)

Somerset House, home of the Queen before the war, had since acquired dark associations for a Royalist. After the King's execution in 1649, his possessions were seized by order of Parliament, and a great auction ('robbery': line 11) was held in Somerset House. In September 1658, Cromwell's embalmed body was moved there from Whitehall, to lie in state like a king. The palaces were deserted by God, says Cowley, as the churches also were (line 2); the misfortunes of Somerset House are compared to the Battle of Naseby (1645), a decisive Royalist defeat (lines 1–16). The house opens on to the Strand, a central artery of the City of London: Cowley calls it a 'channel' (line 33), and his imagery follows the marine connotations of the name ('strand' is sea shore). To the west are the Inns of Court, whose year is divided into terms (line 37). The house backs on to the Thames, where it 'gazes on itself' in the water (lines 33–46: Cowley perhaps intends a complimentary reference to the new suite of state rooms built at the back in 1663–4). It stands at the curve of the river, where 'two joint cities' meet (line 48): the City of London and Westminster, then under separate jurisdiction. To the east, in the City, stands St Paul's Cathedral; to the west is Westminster Abbey, dedicated to St Peter (Paul and Peter were both apostles: line 59). Westminster, home of the court, is power; the City is money (lines 47–60: for the directions 'left' and 'right' in line 54 to work, the house must here be facing the Thames – using its 'other front': line 39). Looking further afield, the house finds its view blocked by a 'wondrous street' (line 63): London Bridge (not Fleet Street), then the only bridge over the Thames, and a busy street. The unseen 'guard of ships' is probably the King's Yard, near Lower Deptford (lines 61–8: in making the ships afraid of fire, Cowley was prophetic – in June 1667, the Dutch sailed up the Medway to the docks at Chatham, and burned three of the ships there). The Thames is impeded by the bridge, which had nineteen arches (line 72), but runs smoothly thereafter on its way to Whitehall (the 'white palace': line 77). Both ships and bridge represent the King's power, as it extends over the 'main' or sea: he has influence abroad ('lays laws') through his navy, as he controls the Thames with the bridge (lines 77–8: for naval activities at the end of 1664, compare Waller, 'Instructions to a Painter'). In the midst of the naval panegyric comes a touch of pathos: Somerset House, with the other great London palaces, stands on the north bank; opposite, on the south bank, was a notorious area of slum housing ('cabanes' in line 87 are cottages) – an opportunity for the Queen Mother's charity, as she is no haughty 'virtuoso' (line 85: a word recently introduced to describe one with superior taste – or confident of being so). In its closing lines, the house offers a quiet warning: continued happiness depends on learning from the past – the Civil War and its aftermath (line 104: 'may' in line 105 means 'may they').

The Complaint

Verses. A debate, not really resolved, between two self-images: Cowley the unworldly poet, and Cowley the loyal courtier. The poem is a reminder that Cowley's much-vaunted love for the secluded life was only half the story. The profoundest moments are those that recognize the ambiguity: Cowley is a 'demi-votary' (line 138) – only half of a religious follower; and his Muse comes 'at once to pity and revile' (line 100).

The setting is Cambridge, where Cowley had a fellowship until Puritan domination there drove him to Oxford. Even the willow is 'careful' – full of care (line 5). Here the Muse of poetry appears, as to Pindar (translated by Cowley) at his home near the Ismenus, and reproaches Cowley as a prodigal son: like the biblical original, he has been reduced to feeding on husks (lines 24–7; compare Luke 15:11 ff.), although he has received as much as any of the nine Muses have given anyone. In abandoning poetry, he has gained nothing, even though the 'public storm' (line 52) of the Civil War has ceased. Biblical parallels knock the point home. As a sign of his divine mission as leader of the Israelites, Gideon asked that a lamb's fleece should remain dry while the ground around it was covered with dew (Judges 6:39–40); the benevolence of Charles II has brought nourishment to everything except poetry. Laban promised Jacob his daughter Rachel as a reward for seven years' service, but in fact gave him her older sister Leah instead, imposing a further seven years for Rachel (Genesis 29:16–28); Cowley here refers to his hopes for the Mastership of the Savoy, awarded instead to Dr Henry Killigrew. The year of the Restoration, when rewards were handed out to the King's old friends, is compared to the days when God fed the Israelites in the desert with manna (Exodus 16:13–36): very little of it, however, reached Cowley (lines 62–98). Cowley replies by blaming the Muse for his failed career. Poetry has prevented him from flourishing, just as fairies were said to cause grass to wither where they danced (line 120; compare 'fairy rings'). Nothing will bring back ('reduce' in its Latin sense: line 126) the mind as it was. Cowley's 'error' (line 137) is to be half-hearted: the final biblical example is the story of Ananias and his wife Sapphira, who gave only part of the proceeds of a sale to the apostles; scolded by St Peter for defrauding God, they both dropped down dead (Acts 5:1–10). After that, the self-consoling of the last stanza might seem a little weak.

Ode: Upon Dr Harvey

Verses. William Harvey (1578–1657) was physician successively to James I and Charles I, whom he attended at the Battle of Edgehill (1642). He is best known for his discovery of the circulation of the blood (his exposition was first published in 1628); his last important work, on the generation of animals, was published in 1651. He and Cowley were both in Oxford from 1642 to 1644.

The poem begins with an extraordinary reworking of the myth of Daphne and her pursuer, the god Apollo (for the basis of which, see Waller, 'The Story of Phoebus and Daphne Applied'). Nature, tracked by Harvey, is seen as a woman in flight; after failing to escape him in the 'fibres of a plant' (line 11), she tries to take refuge in the 'purple' 'Meander' – that is, the winding river of the blood (lines 18–19). There 'well-purgèd ears' (line 22: that is, receptive ones: Cowley is translating a phrase from Horace, Epistle I. 1, lines 11–12) hear her boast: the heart is a safe refuge, defended by its 'wall' (line 28) – the septum between the right and left ventricles. However, unlike Proteus, the sea-god (line 33), she cannot escape, even by changing her form. In the third stanza, Cowley turns to Harvey's work on embryology: the 'living buildings' of line 46 are bodies; 'implied' in line 47 presumably has the sense 'employed'. Nature, at first a pagan nymph, is treated with Christian dignity in the fourth stanza as the Book of the Creatures – a source of knowledge about God, complementary to the Bible; relying on second-hand information is compared to reading biblical commentaries ('comments': line 57) instead of the text. Harvey's original work has cured medicine itself (lines 67 ff.: 'purging' is a medical term). The last stanza mixes praise for Harvey with reproach of the 'age' (line 77): his failure to publish much after 1651 is blamed on the Civil War, which has thus lost the equivalent of the Golden Fleece, brought home after a hard quest by the Greek hero Jason. To reconstruct Harvey's work is harder than to repair St Paul's – a task attempted sporadically from the 1560s; in 1666, the old building would at last be destroyed in the Great Fire.

Ode: 'Acme and Septimius'

Verses. An expanded translation of Catullus 45: very much Cowley's most erotic poem. The opening of the Latin epigraph quoted here is literally translated: 'Septimius holding his love Acme on his lap.' Septimius means 'nothing less than rest' – sleep is the last thing he intends. Sneezing is an omen (line 16): here a good one, as the god blesses their love. 'Little Loves' (line 17) are cupids, little love-gods.

The Country Mouse

Verses; reprinted in the essay 'Of Agriculture' in 1668. Horace's satire praises the quiet life at his Sabine farm, as opposed to the crowds and clamour of Rome; at a modest Sabine dinner party, one of the guests tells this fable – the only part of the satire that Cowley translates. In 1666, this was included in a composite volume edited by Alexander Brome, with a translation of the first half by Cowley's friend, Thomas Sprat; in the next century, Swift and Pope also translated half of the poem each. In a letter to a friend, Cowley describes himself as 'a Mouse of the the wiser kind'. Compare the fable in the second half of Oldham's 'A Satire Addressed to a Friend'.

The poem pits two ideas of the Hellenistic philosophy Epicureanism against each other: the debased, popular conception of self-indulgence represented by the 'nice' or choosy City Mouse (line 26), and the more authentic ideal of simplicity and modest contentment represented by the Country Mouse at the beginning (and considered at length in Cowley's *Essays*). Cowley expands the Latin, adding many little comic touches. Mock-epic dignity is provided by the passages of grandiloquent verse: the sea-nymph Thetis here represents the sea, which turns red ('blushed') with the setting sun, represented by Phoebus (lines 53–5); Cynthia represents the moon, and the 'meridies' is literally the 'midday of the night' – that is, midnight (lines 68–9); the mice have their own 'genius' or guardian spirit (line 25). When the Country Mouse panics, he echoes Luke 23:30 and Revelation 6:16, where it is predicted that mankind will call on rocks, hills and mountains to fall on them and cover them (line 91). But the two are English mice, as well as epic or tragic heroes: the tapestries they find are from Mortlake in south-west London, where there was a famous factory (line 65); 'Fitches', 'peason' and 'tares' (lines 15, 95) are kinds of pea that grow wild in the English countryside; and even the sophisticated 'haut-goust' (a French word for 'savoury') turns out to be the 'swerd' or rind of bacon (lines 18–19). Cowley gives them one word all of their own: Bishop Hurd, one of Cowley's eighteenth-century editors, was the first to point out that the word 'belighted' (line 10) is formed by Cowley on the analogy of 'benighted': '*to be overtaken by light*, being to a mouse, whose journey of course is performed in the dark, what the being overtaken by *night* is, to a man, who travels by day' (R. Hurd (ed.) *Select Works in Verse and Prose, of Mr A. Cowley* (1722), II, p. 170).

The Country Life

Works. This, taken from the essay 'Of Agriculture', is an expanded translation of Cowley's own Latin from the beginning of Book IV of the *Libri Plantarum*, given below. The English and the Latin were published posthumously. The story of Abdolominus comes from Quintus Curtius (*Alexander*, Book IV); the story of Aglaüs comes from the Elder Pliny (*Natural History*, Book VII), and Valerius Maximus (*Memorable Deeds and Sayings*, Book VII). The 'Corycian yeoman' (line 12) is the old man described in Virgil, Georgic IV. 125 ff., who lives cheerfully on very little. The poem is a pastiche of classical verse (the Latin has echoes of Ovid), and the settings are Greek. King Gyges communicates with Apollo at Delphi through the oracle, the god's usual means of speaking to men (lines 27 ff.). Arcadia, a region in the central Peloponnese, was associated by Classical poets and their imitators with an idyllic pastoral life (lines 44–5). 'Sopho's town' (line 46) is better known as Psophis.

LIBRI PLANTARUM

Book IV

Poemata. Cowley's original Latin from the beginning of Book IV of the *Libri Plantarum*.

Upon the Chair Made out of Sir Francis Drake's Ship

Verses. This is Cowley's second (and much shorter) poem about this chair, which is still in the Bodleian Library; he wrote this shorter poem also in Latin, and both versions, on a plate, are attached to the chair. The voyages of discovery always excited him: Book V of the *Libri Plantarum* contains a long description of Columbus's voyage. Pythagoras (line 3) was a Greek philosopher who taught that the soul at death passes into another body, and claimed to remember many of his own past lives. The ship's experiential knowledge and its bodily transformation make it 'Pythagorean'. 'Station' in line 8 means 'situation'; 'estate' means 'state of life'. In the last lines of the Latin extract from Book IV of the *Libri Plantarum* (above), Cowley asks a quiet ending for the 'tossed ship' of his own life.

EDMUND WALLER

The following abbreviations have been used for the texts on which these poems have been based. In all but two cases the text is the last published in Waller's lifetime or the first published after it: the exceptions are 'Sir John and Lady Denham', taken from a manuscript copy, and 'Instructions to a Painter', which was published later in a greatly expanded form.

MS: University of Nottingham Library, MS PwV 431
Instructions: Instructions to a Painter for the Drawing of a Picture of the State and Posture of the English Forces at Sea, under the Command of his Royal Highness, in the Conclusion of the year 1664 (1665)
Masque: The New Masque for 'The Maid's Tragedy' (?1683)
Poems: Poems, etc. (1686)
Second Part: The Second Part of Mr Waller's Poems (1690)

Of His Majesty's Receiving the News of the Duke of Buckingham's Death

Poems; first published 1645. George Villiers, first Duke of Buckingham, favourite first of James I and then of his son Charles I, but highly unpopular with the country at large, was assassinated by John Felton, a former soldier he had commanded, in August 1628. The news was brought to the King while he was at prayer. According to Clarendon, he expressed no emotion until the prayers were finished, whereupon he lamented 'with much passion'; but his initial self-control provoked a rumour that he was not sorry to be rid of Buckingham. Waller's poem was perhaps intended to scotch the rumour.

Waller draws his flattering imagery from the Old Testament and from classical mythology. The 'sacred wrestler' in line 3 is Jacob, who wrestled with an unknown man 'until the break of day', and would not let him go until he received a blessing from the stranger (Genesis 32:24–30). David (line 27) grieved for the death of his friend Jonathan, but allowed Ziba, a deceitful servant of Jonathan's family, to share the inheritance with Mephibosheth, Jonathan's lame son (2 Samuel 16:1–4; 19:24–30); Waller marks the contrast with Charles, who took Buckingham's son into the royal nursery to be brought up with his own children. In line 10, the King is compared favourably with Achilles, the 'pattern' or model hero in Homer's *Iliad*, who responded with violent grief to the death of his friend Patroclus at the hand of the Trojan prince Hector (Book XVIII). The prince in line 18 is the Greek King Agamemnon, ordered by a goddess to sacrifice his daughter Iphigenia in return for a wind to sail to Troy; the 'famous painter' in line 17 (as Waller's first commentator, Fenton, pointed out in *Works*) is

Timanthes, whose picture of the scene showed the other characters in different degrees of distress, but concealed Agamemnon's face in the folds of his drapery. Had Timanthes seen Charles, says Waller, he would have had a model for such 'private sorrow' (line 18). The remaining classical references are more surprising. Lines 23 – 6 allude to two boys loved and mourned by the god Apollo (Phoebus): Cyparissus, who grieved himself to death for the loss of his pet deer ('heart' is a pun: 1645 – 68 editions spell it 'hart'); and Hyacinthus, accidentally killed by the god himself with a discus (Apollo's 'fate' in line 25 is his immortality). 'Compressed' in line 37 means 'raped' – a typical fate of those loved by the pagan gods. A contemporary reader, remembering old rumours about Buckingham's relations with King James, might have found the Cyparissus and Hyacinthus images rather piquant.

To Van Dyck

Poems; first published in 1645. Anthony Van Dyck (1599 – 1641) settled in England in the 1630s, was knighted by Charles I (a keen connoisseur of the visual arts), and became the favourite painter of the court and the nobility. Compare Cowley's poem on his death. Characteristically, Waller turns praise of the painter's skill into courtliness towards his model: the assertion that Van Dyck could not produce a likeness 'at one assay' (line 27: that is, on one attempt) is an excuse for gallant explanations. 'So' in line 25 means 'as long as'; 'the hazard of his fame' in line 34 means 'at the risk of his reputation' (either for morality, or for artistic skill – since seeing her so often means he needed more time). In Greek myth, Prometheus (line 50), himself an immortal, stole fire from the gods to give to men. It may be significant that Cowley followed the Van Dyck elegy in his 1656 volume with a short poem on a bad picture of Prometheus.

The Story of Phoebus and Daphne Applied

Poems; first published in 1645. When Apollo, god of poets ('the inspirèd train': line 1), pursued the nymph Daphne, she was rescued by Diana, the virgin goddess, who transformed her into a laurel. The laurel wreath is the victor's traditional reward. Chernaik, *Poetry of Limitation*, compares Waller's poem with Marvell, 'The Garden' (pp. 85–6); Waller liked it enough to produce a Latin translation. Thorn Drury, *Poems*, is sardonic: 'if one is disposed to take offence . . . it can only be said that so far at least his remarkable confidence has been justified' (I, p. xxx). The anonymous author of the 1711 memoir reacted very differently: 'This is one of the most gallant and best-turned copies of verses in the English tongue; and that which he applies to himself, with a modest and just boldness, can never be enough admired' (p. xiii). 'Lawrel', the old alternative spelling of 'laurel', is an anagram of 'Waller', used in flattering contemporary epigrams about him, and probably in his mind here.

The Self Banished

Poems; first published in 1645. A fine example of Waller's ability to develop elaborate argument in simple language and a strict form. A musical setting by Henry Lawes was published in *Airs and Dialogues* (1653). In lines 5–7, 'everything' is the subject, 'Your form' the object of 'bring'; 'Who' in line 9 stands for 'he who'; the 'rage' in line 15 is a fever. The last stanza has a twist: keeping his vow to stay away (explained earlier as self-protection) is in fact a necessary part of his courtship, as it confirms that he will keep his vow to love her.

Song ('Go, lovely rose')

Poems; first published in 1645. This is perhaps the most famous example in English verse of the rose as reminder of time's threat to love – a theme which has been traced back to Ausonius in the fourth century AD It is discussed at length by Chernaik, *Poetry of Limitation*, pp. 107 ff. The famous musical setting by Lawes was first published in the second volume of *Airs and Dialogues* (1655). Ezra Pound used this poem, published in the middle of a war, as the basis of his own 'Envoi (1919)' – a title that marks the end of another; the two are considered together in the last chapter of Geoffrey Hill, *The Enemy's Country* (Oxford, 1991).

The Battle of the Summer Islands

Poems; first published in 1645. The Bermudas were known also as the Summer(s) or Somers Islands after Sir George Somers (spelling variable), shipwrecked there *en route* for Virginia. Thorn Drury, *Poems*, notes that there is no evidence that Waller visited the islands himself; in June 1628, however, he was appointed to a parliamentary committee to consider a petition from the settlers against a proposed raise in the tobacco tax. The paradisal description here may be compared with travellers' accounts – for example, *The True Travels of Captain John Smith* (1624), on which Waller was perhaps drawing. The poem is a short mock-epic in three cantos: the second and third cantos describe the fight between two whales and a boat of Bermudan fishermen. For a discussion of this first canto, and a comparison of it with Marvell's 'Bermudas', see Røstvig, *The Happy Man*, I, pp. 150–52. Thorn Drury suggests that the 'huge sea-monsters' of Marvell's poem may allude to the whale fight Waller describes (*Poems*, II, p. 180).

As a mock-epic, the poem begins with an invocation to the Roman goddess of warfare (line 1). Other classical references suggest both Paradise and its loss: the golden apples of the Hesperides (line 8) were stolen by Hercules as one of his Twelve Labours; 'fierce Cato' (line 22), according to Plutarch's *Life* of him, threw figs from Carthage on to the floor of the Senate in order to convince his countrymen that the place's natural wealth made it a threat, which Rome must destroy. The vegetation includes the palmetto (a small species of palm: line 17), the pineapple (line 33), and the palm-christ (castor-oil plant: line 52). The 'blest tenant' is a settler; the 'landlords' are the Somers Island Company, which was granted a charter in 1612 (lines 30–31). The islands were uninhabited before the Europeans arrived; very small numbers of the native populations of other colonies were imported before the mid-1640s, but it is likely that the 'savages' in the last line originate in Waller's imagination.

'Mould' in line 31 seems to mean 'style, mode'. 'At once ... at once', in line 43, a favourite construction of Waller's, means that the two actions happen simultaneously. His 'vein' (line 65) is his poetic gift.

To Phyllis

Poems; first published in 1645. In the poetic miscellany *Wits Recreations* (1645), unauthorized by Waller, this poem is entitled 'The Cunning Court-esan', and is given to a woman to speak ('Phyllis' becomes 'Sir'). That change of title neatly reveals the extent to which *carpe diem* ('seize the day') was an erotic theme available to women. With the last line, compare the last line of 'Of English Verse'.

To my Lord of Falkland

Poems; first published in 1645. Lucius Cary, second Viscount Falkland, took part in the expedition against the Scots in 1639; the Earl of Holland was appointed General of the Horse. Cowley wrote a poem for Falkland's safe return from this expedition. Falkland, a man of culture and generosity, made a great impression on his contemporaries: Clarendon, his close friend, writes of him with reverence in his *History of the Rebellion*. His death at the Battle of Newbury (1643), widely believed to be quasi-suicidal, brings Cowley's epic on the Civil War to an abrupt and anguished stop.

Waller takes examples of conflict from Greek myth and the Old Testament. In lines 5–10, he alludes to the war waged unsuccessfully by the Giants, monstrous beings of great strength, against the Olympian gods (Fenton, *Works*, p. l, quotes Horace, Ode III. 4, who emphasizes the role of Apollo, and his paradoxical nature as both bearer of the 'silver bow' and patron god of poets – the 'spring' in Waller's poem is on Mount Helicon, home of those 'sacred virgins' the Muses (lines 7–8), and its water bestowed poetic inspiration). In lines 26–8, the 'fair Hebrew' is Rebecca, pregnant with Esau and Jacob (Genesis 25:22–3). The explanation offered for their conflict by the Lord is not perhaps as comforting as Waller suggests: 'Two nations are in thy womb, and two manner of people shall be separated from thy bowels; and the one people shall be stronger than the other people; and the elder shall serve the younger.'

In line 14, the reference is to the ivy wreath of the poet and the laurel (bay) wreath of the victor.

For Drinking of Healths

Poems; first published in 1645. The nearest Waller ever came to a 'Cavalier' poem of self-conscious revelling (a 'health' is a toast). Drink is here easily associated with love (deserted) and friendship (defended by force). Ariadne, who had helped the Greek hero Theseus to overcome the Minotaur, was deserted by him and then carried off by Bacchus, the god of wine (Phoebus is significant here as the god of poetry ('numbers': line 14)). The 'title to our blood' (line 16) is an entitlement to have it shed.

Thorn Drury, *Poems,* I, pp. 89–90, prints, from a manuscript owned by the Waller family, a version of this poem headed 'An answeare to on that writ against Healths', which is sixteen lines longer than any version printed in Waller's lifetime. The first six lines appear before the present text:

> And is antiquity of no more force!
> Whoe'er opposed that ancient friendly course,
> And free expression of our absent love,
> Against the custom of all nations strove
> And lost his labour, it does still prevail,
> And shall, while there is friendship, wine, or ale.

and the last ten after it:

> 'Twere slender kindness that would not dispense
> With health itself, to breed a confidence
> Of true love in a friend, and he that quits
> Each custom which the rude plebeian gets,
> For his reserv'dness will too dearly pay,
> Employ the night and loose the cheerful day:
> The burnished face oft decked with hoary hairs
> Shows drinking brings no death, but to our cares.
> Who with a full red countenance ends his days,
> He sets like Phoebus and discerns his bays.

Of the Marriage of the Dwarfs

Poems; first published in 1645. Richard Gibson (1615–90), one of Charles I's court dwarfs, married Anne Shepherd, another dwarf, in a ceremony attended by the King and Queen. Court dwarfs seem to have been a favoured subject with poets, as with painters: William Davenant wrote a mock-epic, 'Jeffereidos', on the exploits of Jeffrey Hudson, an exact contemporary of Gibson, also apparently under four feet high. Waller's mockery is less raucous, more whimsical. The couple are a little Adam and Eve, 'Beneath . . . all care'; (lines 3–12); the third stanza shifts to their perspective, in which their larger contemporaries are monsters: Galatea (line 16) was a shepherdess, loved in vain by the giant Cyclops Polyphemus (Theocritus, Idyll XI). Waller's daughter Dorothy was a dwarf.

From a Child

Poems; first published in 1645. In aristocratic families, children were all dressed in the same way, by women, until the age of six or seven, when little boys were put into breeches and transferred to the care of men. In this slightly uncomfortable poem, a boy, still dressed without differential of sex ('weed' is clothing: line 8), expresses stately admiration for an adult woman; it provides an unusual variant on that favourite contemporary subject, a man's love for a very young girl.

On a Girdle

Poems; first published in 1645. The 'pale' in line 6 is an enclosure; 'dear' is a pun – the girdle becomes a deer-park (compare Shakespeare, *Venus and Adonis*, lines 230–31).

The Apology of Sleep

Poems; first published in 1645. The lady here is Charles I's Queen, Henrietta Maria. Hammond finds this poem 'uncomfortable in its absolute refusal to consider how fragile the court's position has become' (*Fleeting Things*, p. 35). In lines 31–2, Sleep, the narrator, recalls the scene in the *Iliad*, Book XIV (by Homer – the 'Maeonian') in which the goddess Hera induces the god of sleep to work on her husband Zeus (Jove in Latin) so that she has a chance to redress the action of the Trojan War in favour of the Greeks. The 'spotless skies' (line 25) – unspotted by clouds – belong to Egypt, whose fertility depends upon the seasonal overflowing of the Nile; Phoebus here features as the god of the sun. Compare 'A Panegyric to my Lord Protector', lines 53–4.

[At Penshurst]

Poems; first published in 1645, where 'Sacharissa' (line 1) is called 'Doro-
thea'. The original was Lady Dorothy Sidney, eldest daughter of the Earl
of Leicester, whose family home was Penshurst. Waller wrote a very
charming letter on her marriage in 1639 in the form of a mock-curse:

may she live to be very old, and yet seem young, be told so by her glass, and have
no aches to inform her of the truth: and when she shall appear to be mortal, may
her Lord not mourn for her, but go hand in hand with her to that place where we
are told there is neither marrying nor giving in marriage, that being there divorced
we may all have an equal interest in her again (printed in the 1711 *Life* and in Thorn
Drury, *Poems*, I, p. xxix).

A less charming conversation between them in later years is also reported
by the 1711 anonymous memoir: 'she . . . asked him in raillery, "When,
Mr Waller, will you write such fine verses upon me again?" "Oh, Madam,"
said he, "when your ladyship is as young again."' Here he draws on Ben
Jonson's well-known poem 'To Penshurst', but where Jonson concentrates
on the place, Waller uses it as a means to flatter Sacharissa: she is the local
goddess, the equal of Orpheus and Amphion (heroes with wonderful,
attracting powers over nature). '[O]bsequious' in line 16 means 'dutiful'.
Ingeniously, Waller associates himself with her noble family: he is another
Sir Philip Sidney, kinsman to her but fellow-sufferer with him as a poet in
love. The tree planted on the day of Sidney's birth and carved over by
lovers is celebrated by Jonson too. Lines 27–30 are not quite clear: 'they'
seems to refer to the evidence of love that is written into the tree bark,
guaranteed immortality by the astral powers associated with Sidney. '[S]tars'
(line 28) are especially appropriate as Sidney's sonnets are addressed to
'Stella', the Latin for 'Star'.

Song ('Behold the brand of Beauty tossed')

Poems; first published in 1645. For comparison with this delicate poem, see
Richard Lovelace, 'Gratiana dancing and singing'. The reference in line
14 is to the music of the spheres – the harmony supposed to be produced
by the heavenly bodies together, as each made one note while moving in
its orbit. (See also note to Cowley, *Davideis*: Book I [Music].) 'Numbers'
(line 16), here means music.

A la Malade

Poems; first published in 1645: 'To the sick lady'. The identity of Amoret has been disputed: Fenton, *Works*, p. xlii, citing Waller's friend the second Duke of Buckingham, claimed that she was Lady Sophia Murray, a participant in Waller's ill-fated plot; Thorn Drury, *Poems*, II, p. 179, following a note in a Waller family manuscript, prefers Lady Anne Cavendish, later Lady Rich, for whose early death Waller wrote an elegy which promised to commemorate her 'sacred friendship' with Sacharissa. Here he presents her sickness as an attempt by Heaven to woo her – an attempt which suggests that the gifts formerly showered on her (beauty, etc.) had the usual lover's purpose of deceit (lines 3–6). Her soul, more visible through the wasting of the body (lines 21–4), is compared, in a bold and disturbing image, to the bodies of nymphs in flight from would-be lovers: their *déshabille* stimulates their pursuers' desire ('flame') and haste (lines 25–30).

To the Mutable Fair

Poems; first published in 1645. A poem about changefulness, in both beloved and lover. He begins apparently in despair at her inconstancy, but soon it becomes clear that he is fascinated by it, and the last paragraph reaches a subtle compromise: she will be immortalized, but with 'blame' (line 61), provided she holds his interest by deceiving him. The imagery lightens the poem still further: 'make a stoop' (line 16) is a term from falconry; the goddess Juno made a likeness of herself out of cloud to escape rape by Ixion (lines 31 ff.). The transformations in lines 45 ff. thwarted the god of Apollo in pursuit of Daphne, the river god Alpheus in pursuit of Arethusa, and the god Neptune in pursuit of Coronis (for the first, see 'The Story of Apollo and Daphne Applied'; for all three, Ovid, *Metamorphoses*, Books I, V and II). Lines 13–14 refer to a famous episode of Cervantes' novel *Don Quixote*: the deluded knight attacks a windmill believing it to be a giant (I, chapter viii).

In Answer of Sir John Suckling's Verses

Poems; first published in 1645. After Ben Jonson's translation of 'Foeda est in coetu', a short Latin poem then believed to be by Petronius, English poems 'against fruition' (sexual consummation) became quite common in the seventeenth century: Suckling's 'Against Fruition', the 'Con.' part of this exchange, was not published until 1646, along with another piece on the same theme and with the same title; Henry Bold wrote another verse-response. Compare Cowley, 'Against Fruition', and Oldham, 'A

Fragment of Petronius, Paraphrased'. By the standards of the genre, Suck-ling's poem is well-mannered (compare Oldham's 'squirt': line 5); Waller politely deflects his one brutal image by making a distinction between ploughing, the work of 'hinds' (labourers), and 'nobler tillage' (lines 33–8). 'Pro' and 'Con' (short for contra) are the Latin for 'For' and 'Against'. Anchises (line 36) was a mortal lover of the goddess Venus: he, not her husband, the god Vulcan, was the father of the hero Aeneas. Nepenthe (line 14) is a plant traditionally supposed to drive away sorrow. An 'heroic tale' (line 45) is an epic.

On Mr John Fletcher's Plays

Poems; first published in 1645, and reprinted in the Beaumont and Fletcher Folio *Comedies and Tragedies* of 1647 (from which this edition, like Thorn Drury's *Poems*, takes the second line). John Fletcher (1579–1625) remained a highly popular playwright throughout the century. After the Restoration, Waller wrote a new fifth act and a masque for *The Maid's Tragedy*: see the extract in this volume from 'The New Masque for *The Maid's Tragedy*'. The brave Melantius and the tragic Aspasia (lines 8–12) are characters from this play (the 'inimitable Maid' – line 14); *The Scornful Lady* (line 16) is another play by Beaumont and Fletcher. The references to clothes in lines 5–6 and 7 ff. are contradictory: Waller first says that Fletcher's plays, a credit to his own and an entertainment for the present generation, are the only ones popular enough to pay for good costumes for their actors; then that the audience will see their own clothes on the stage (in fact actors' costumes were usually cast-offs). The comparison at the end is rather compressed: the sense is that the contest is best not when all the combatants are nearly equal, but when an outsider steps in and raises the standard. The others, however, are reduced to despair; hence Fletcher has spoiled the game, as well as improving it. This ambiguous attitude to the achievements of the previous age can be found in Waller's contemporary, Dryden: see his *Essay of Dramatic Poesy* (1668).

A Panegyric to my Lord Protector

First published in 1655, by two separate publishers. With Thorn Drury, *Poems*, this text follows the one 'printed by Thomas Newcomb'; like the two published in 1690, this does not have four-line stanzas, as the other 1655 edition and all editions after 1711 have (including Thorn Drury). Manuscript evidence suggests that both forms were current; the non-stanzaic form, chosen here, reads very differently from the other – more fluent, less aphoristic. The paragraph breaks here are a compromise between the 1655 breaks and those in *The Maid's Tragedy Altered* (1690), which are slightly different. The other non-stanzaic copies I have seen have no paragraphs.

The poem eulogizes Oliver Cromwell, who had become Lord Protector in 1653, ending four years of parliamentary sovereignty. His government was marked by tolerant but formidable rule at home, and an aggressive, global foreign policy. Thorn Drury prints a letter from him to Waller, thanking him for a poem of praise – presumably this one; Royalists greeted it with a fusillade of angry parodies. The year 1655 was especially hard for them: Penruddock's Rising, a Royalist conspiracy in the West Country, was suppressed, and led to harsher measures from the government (Cowley was arrested). 'Bridle faction' (line 2) was a shocking subject of praise for an ex-Cavalier, as was Cromwell's 'blood' or lineage (line 128 – a part of the poem attacked with particular ferocity).

The political scene is complex. The 'unwilling Scotch' (line 16), also called Caledonians (line 82), who had supported Charles II (on their own terms), were defeated with him at the Battle of Worcester in 1651; Scotland was united with England by legislation in 1654. In 1640 they had marched into England: Waller says that they were bribed to do so ('foreign gold': line 87), and that they will remain henceforth behind Hadrian's Wall (line 85). Ireland, conquered by means of a bloody campaign in 1649, was reorganized through heavy confiscation and colonization in the 1650s: it was the English settlers who were granted representation in the Parliament of the Three Nations in 1654 to which Scotland is also 'preferred' (advanced) (lines 15–16; 89–100). The 'late fight' in line 105, in which the roar of cannons is said to have outstripped the written news – '(preventing posts)': line 106 – is the First Dutch War, which ended in 1653 with the defeat of the Dutch at sea; Cromwell secured an advantageous peace treaty by which British ships were declared supreme in British waters (the 'forests' in line 42 are wooden ships), and the two countries agreed to expel each other's enemies – a blow against conspiring Royalists abroad (lines 101–3).

The classical imagery of the poem is spare and concentrated. The simile in lines 9–12 is a double one: Neptune (line 9), god of the sea, emerges in the *Aeneid*, Book I, to calm the storm which is about to destroy Aeneas; Virgil compares his action to that of a great man who quells a riot by the force of his authority; Waller makes Cromwell a statesman who is like Neptune who is like a statesman. The 'Macedonian' (line 73) is Alexander the Great, who wept at having no more worlds to conquer (compare Plutarch, 'Of Tranquillity and Contentment of Mind') – not realizing, says Waller, that there were more lands, not yet discovered, beyond the ocean (represented by the sea-nymph Thetis). Finally, the Roman analogy which pervades the poem provides Waller with a conveniently complex perspective for Cromwell's controversial career. Julius Caesar, the great military commander who seized political power in a turbulent state, was assassinated by the staunch Republican Brutus (among others); Caesar's death was followed by thirteen years of war and struggle, before his adopted son Octavian (later Augustus) won his victory at Actium. Cromwell has the greatness of Julius (line 149), and the reward of Augustus (line 170), having 'dazzled' those who 'pretended' (aspired: line 139) to continue war. Compare Cowley, 'Brutus'.

The two biblical heroes are chosen for their rise from humble origins. David (line 136), later King of Israel, was discovered by the prophet Samuel while tending sheep (I Samuel 16:11); Joseph (line 188), the eleventh son of Jacob, had a prophetic dream in which the wheat-sheaf he was binding stood upright, while those of his brothers stood round it and bowed (Genesis 37:7).

Prologue for the Lady Actors

Second Part. Actresses appeared on the English stage for the first time at the end of 1660; here they address the King in the audience. Waller's gallant defence of their sexual virtue contrasts pleasingly with everything known about most of them. This poem was also published in *The Maid's Tragedy Altered* (1690), without lines 3–4.

On St James's Park

Poems. Extensive changes – 'brave alterations', as Pepys called them – were made to the Park between 1660 and 1662. They included a canal, a menagerie, and a 'Mall' – an alley for the new game of pell mell, an early form of croquet imported from France. This poem first appeared as a broadside in 1661; the canal had not yet frozen enough to support skaters (line 24), but on 1 December 1662, Pepys and Evelyn both saw them there.

Waller depicts the park as a second Eden with pagan embellishments (lines 1–6): the water holds nymphs sent by Thetis, a sea-goddess (lines 38–9), while the animals of the menagerie remind him of the Ark, and of 'Peter's sheet' – the vessel that descends before the apostle in Acts 10:11–12, 'as if it had been a great sheet knit at the corners', containing animals of all kinds for him to eat (lines 43–4). The park's orderliness also suggests those mythic harmonizers Orpheus and Amphion (lines 15–16: see '[At Penshurst]'): it is as one with special power over nature that Charles II enters the poem (line 58). In the second half, the trees appear as giants, natural forces to be tamed (lines 69–70: compare 'To my Lord of Falkland', lines 9–10), and Charles appears in his role as prudent, human King, with serious duties: the 'first kings' of line 71 suggest the ancient Roman King Numa, who was said to be counselled by a wise nymph, Egeria. The buildings near the park have complex associations. Whitehall (line 87) was built by the 'prelate' Wolsey, but taken by Henry VIII after his fall; Waller compares its 'fortune' to that of the Capitol (line 88), built by King Tarquin, who was subsequently chased from Rome. He says nothing of its later notoriety, as the scene of the execution of Charles I; but after 'that antique pile', Westminster Abbey (line 91), come the Houses of Parliament (line 99), which are blamed (lightly) for the Civil War. The King's gaze at last reaches Westminster Hall (line 105), seat of the four Courts of Justice; as he meditates regally, the poet projects him back into myth, but myth now transformed. As Fenton notes in *Works*, a star had been observed at about noon as Charles I was returning from St Paul's after a ceremony of thanksgiving for the birth of his first son. Hercules, or Alcides (line 124), was conceived by Alcmena after a night with Jupiter that lasted twice as long as an ordinary night; Charles II's birth, less scandalously, is marked by a night which is like a day (lines 129–30).

The first edition of the poem was revised by Waller as it was printed: lines 31–2 and 35–6 were added during the revision; lines 95–6 were added in 1664; after line 66, the unrevised and revised 1661 versions have an extra couplet:

> May that ill fate my enemies befall
> To stand before his anger or his ball.

In line 52, 'July' rhymes with 'duly' – the older pronunciation.

Instructions to a Painter

Instructions. The version given here is the earliest, now very rare: a broadside, entered in the Stationer's Register in November 1664. The subject of dispute was the trading rights of England and Holland – already the subject of an expensive war under Cromwell's Protectorate. At the point marked by this version, war had not yet been declared, but the English fleet had set sail, and some skirmishing had begun. Waller expanded the poem enormously in the following year, after the brilliant victory at the Battle of Lowestoft in June 1665. The expanded version inspired a series of vicious parodies, one at least by Marvell, as the Second Dutch War turned into an English fiasco.

Waller's chief hero is James, Duke of York, Lord High Admiral and brother of the King; 'abroad' (line 11) under duress, between the early years of the Civil War and the Restoration, he had earned an impressive reputation as a military commander, fighting for other European powers. The action fancifully described in lines 29 – 46 took place between July and November 1664. In July, the Dutch merchant ships were directed to make a long detour round the coast of Scotland in order to avoid the English fleet in the Channel (lines 34–6). In November, more than one hundred and thirty Dutch merchant ships were captured; Waller repeats the common libel that the Dutch are a nation of drunkards (compare 'Dutch courage'), and imagines the English drinking the wine they have captured (lines 41–6). In the same month, Sir Thomas Allen concluded a peace-treaty with the Algerines ('Moors'), and in December, he made an attack on the Smyrna fleet (lines 47–54: in fact he made two; the first, unmentioned by Waller, was a failure). Personification of wine as Bacchus (line 41), and Latinizing 'Dutch' to 'Batavian' (line 22), contribute to the atmosphere of almost pageant-like grandeur with which Waller transforms the historical events. 'Preventing' in line 21 means 'coming before' (and thus preventing); the 'Belgian' (line 34) is a citizen of the Low Countries, not distinct here from the Dutch.

Upon Her Majesty's New Buildings at Somerset House

Poems; first published as a broadside in 1665. Henrietta Maria, widow of Charles I, returned to England from her long exile in France in 1660 and set about restoring Somerset House, the palace in the Strand which had been hers before the Civil War, but had later been given by Parliament to Cromwell. Compare Cowley, 'On the Queen's Repairing Somerset House'. She did not stay for long: in June 1665, she returned to France, where she died four years later. The paragraph breaks here follow Thorn Drury, *Poems*, rather than the seventeenth-century texts.

[Sir John and Lady Denham]

MS. This malicious little squib was first published by Thorn Drury in *A Little Ark* (1921). Sir John Denham (1615–69)), veteran Cavalier-poet, caused his contemporaries cruel mirth in 1665 by his marriage to Margaret Brooke, many years his junior, and soon to become the mistress of the Duke of York – if Waller's insinuations are correct, she was so already. *Cooper's Hill* (briefly discussed in the note on Cowley, 'On the Queen's Repairing Somerset House') has always been Denham's best-known poem; in it he gives generous praise to a poem by Waller on St Paul's. The present piece depends on two facts: Margaret Brooke's name, and Denham's lameness (which seems to have contributed to a general idea that he was much older than in fact he was).

Of English Verse

Poems; first published in 1668. The primary idea of this poem – that English is a rapidly-changing language which soon loses its currency – was to be something of an obsession in the next fifty years: compare Sir William Temple, 'On Ancient and Modern Learning' (1690), and Pope, 'An Essay on Criticism' (1711), lines 480 ff. Not everyone, however, was so pessimistic: Pope's contemporary, Bishop Atterbury, in his copy of Waller, quotes a passage from *The Knight's Tale* to demonstrate its modernity, and asserts that Waller did not read Chaucer 'with attention'; the Introduction to *Second Part*, generally thought to be Atterbury's, remarks that 'though English be mouldering stone . . . he has certainly picked out the best of a bad quarry'. In 1700, Dryden published 'translations' from Chaucer in his *Fables Ancient and Modern*; the dedicatory poem 'To Her Grace the Duchess of Ormonde' begins with the idea developed by Waller in lines 17 ff.: that the poet immortalized women he loved. According to the Preface to the *Fables*, Cowley was among those who considered Chaucer 'a dry, old-fashioned wit, not worth receiving'.

Upon the Earl of Roscommon's Translation of Horace, De Arte Poetica

Poems; first published with Roscommon's translation in 1680. Wentworth Dillon, Lord Roscommon (?1633–85), also wrote an original verse-treatise entitled 'An Essay upon Translated Verse', and according to Fenton, (*Works*, p. lxxvii), 'began to form a society for the refining and fixing the standard of our language' with Dryden and others, which – like the Royal Society Committee of which Waller was a member – came to nothing. Oldham praised Roscommon's translation warmly in the Preface to his own attempt.

This poem has a courtly opening: Roscommon is praised for combining Horace's poetic talent with the social nobility of the *Ars Poetica*'s addressee (lines 1–4); but Waller has serious things to say about the direction of English poetry. He refers to the 'wingèd horse', Pegasus (line 11), which struck the spring Hippocrene, source of poetic inspiration, out of Mount Helicon, home of the Muses (line 19); but he argues that Pegasus must be controlled – poetic frenzy ('rage': line 14) alone makes no effect. Beeswax supplies the place of the sun because it is made into candles.

The New Masque for The Maid's Tragedy

Masque. This masque has never been reprinted since its first appearance in an anonymous, undated pamphlet. For Waller and *The Maid's Tragedy*, see note to 'On Mr John Fletcher's Plays'. The masque replaces the original, much longer one, performed in the first act to celebrate the (disastrous) marriage between the hero, Amintor, and the King's mistress, Evadne: the masque characters (Aeolus, god of the winds, and the sea deities) are celebrating a wedding, in the traditional terms of female bashfulness and male persistence. Lines 23–4 are highly characteristic of Waller. The verse will all have been set to music. Waller provided a new, much cheerier last act to the play, in which Amintor is finally reunited with his first love, Aspasia. A 'nereid' is another name for a sea-nymph.

Of Tea, Commended by Her Majesty

Second Part. Charles II's Queen, Catherine of Braganza, is said to have first popularized the drinking of tea in England. Her 'nation' was Portugal, home of such famous explorers as Vasco da Gama, who discovered the eastern route to India round the Cape of Good Hope (lines 4–5).

Of the Last Verses in the Book

First printed in 1686, this is much the best-known of Waller's spiritual poems. It makes its effect with the simplest of images – seas and clouds in the second stanza, the body as house to the soul in the last. The first two lines introduce the poem as one dictated ('indite[d]') because the author is now so weak; this shows how the soul is able to worship when the body fails. In line 4, the sense is 'as the body stoops'. The Virgilian tag comes from Eclogue V. 56: 'he wonders at the threshold of Olympus' (home of the gods).

JOHN OLDHAM

The following abbreviations have been used for the texts on which these poems have been based. In every case but one, the text is the last published in Oldham's lifetime or the first after his death: the exception is the extract from the fourth Jesuit satire, which is taken from the collation prepared by Brooks and Selden.

New Pieces: *Some New Pieces Never before Published* (1681)
Satires: *Satires upon the Jesuits* (1682) (the second edition)
Poems and Translations: *Poems and Translations* (1683)
St Cecilia: *A Second Musical Entertainment performed on St Cecilia's Day* (1685)
Poems: Harold F. Brooks and Raman Selden (eds.), *The Poems of John Oldham* (Oxford, 1987)

SATIRES UPON THE JESUITS

Satire IV [Ignatius in Hell]

Poems. The first of these four satires was first published in a pirated edition in 1679; in 1681 the whole set appeared, and in 1682 a second edition, 'more corrected'. The present text is based on the collation in *Poems.* Oldham was cashing in on the current panic induced by the claims of Titus Oates to have discovered an extensive Popish Plot which threatened the life of the King and the safety of the Protestant religion in England; that Oldham did not seriously believe in it for long is clear from the evasive references in his 'Imitation of Horace, Book I, Satire IX', and 'The Careless Good Fellow' – the first published in the same year as the first edition of the *Satires.* The poems are coarse, and in places vicious; what saves them is their energy, and the outrageous comedy they sometimes achieve. This fourth satire is spoken by St Ignatius Loyola, the founder of the order, who reveals the corruption and treachery of his followers.

In this excerpt, Ignatius passes from holy relics (called by him 'trangums', or worthless bric-à-brac: line 2) to Church teaching and practice – equally worthless. A 'jubilee' (line 9) is a sacred festival (see Leviticus 25:9–31) – the Church declared certain years 'jubilees', on which a general amnesty for sin was declared. Antonio Escobar y Mendoza (1589–1669) was a celebrated Spanish Jesuit, whose work considered ethical cases in a way opponents found specious; the 'Datary' is an officer of the papal court, concerned with the awarding of grants and dispensations (lines 10–11). In their impertinent assumptions of knowledge about Hell (not really a Catholic monopoly), designed to frighten the 'rout', or common people (line 24), the Jesuits find a special place for the Huguenots, or French Protestants (line 21). Their 'Chimaeras', or fantastic fables, include the Roman Catholic doctrines of Limbo and Purgatory – two intermediate states (one permanent, the other transitional) between Heaven and Hell. The 'song' (line 28) is an insulting reference to the sung service for the dead, believed by contemporary Catholics to help the departed soul – provided, says Ignatius, it is not the soul of a pauper caught in a debtors' prison (line 32). The centre of the corruption is the doctrine of indulgences, or remission of punishment by Church authority – a doctrine at first carefully defined and restricted, but always liable to venal abuse. Here Ignatius alludes to the practice of tariffs, financial penalties imposed for particular offences, such as taking bribes ('simony') or pederasty (keeping an 'ingle': line 43). Killing a whole family of non-Catholics, by contrast, is meritorious, and does not require an indulgence (lines 46–7). The passage ends with that favourite Protestant target, transubstantiation: the doctrine that the holy wafer eaten by communicants actually changes its substance to the body of Christ. Ignatius follows the idea to a blasphemously logical conclusion: the wafer is 'preferred' (advanced) to a 'jakes' – a lavatory (lines 68–9).

A Letter from the Country to a Friend in Town

New Pieces. The poem is addressed to Oldham's old friend John Spencer, now a barrister; it is a reply to a poem from him, almost identical in length, copied out by Oldham in his autograph notebook, and printed in *Poems*, pp. 534–41. Spencer had declared his own difficulties in writing verse after the fit of drunken enthusiasm has worn off, offered ideas about the best sort of poem (not obscene, or obscure, or ephemeral, or spiteful), and extravagantly praised his friend; Oldham replies with a full, impetuous account of his own passionate engagement with poetry. Critics have claimed that lines 148–85 are based on the beginning of Dryden's dedication to his play *The Rival Ladies* (1664); whether or not this is so, Oldham's much longer and richer description of an unconscious process is remarkable for its time – or indeed any time.

He begins by comparing himself to the poet Ovid, who, exiled to the Black Sea by Augustus for a mysterious offence, wrote moving verse-epistles to his friends, some thanking them for writing to him (lines 1–14). Ovid is an inspiring force in this poem: in one of his exile-poems (*Tristia*, IV. x), he explains his addiction to writing verse from an early age, and refusal to follow a sensible career in law, like his brother – or like Spencer. Oldham's response to Spencer's encouragement is ambiguous, like his attitude to writing: the praise is welcome, but overwhelming, the equivalent of a mother's accidental rolling on to a baby in her sleep ('over-lay': line 26). Spencer himself, who has offered his own thoughts on the fashionable, elusive ideal of 'Wit' (line 41), is enviable for his fluency – he needs no anxious effort ('want no care': line 50), and has no 'strangury' (line 45: literally, a disease restricting the passage of urine); on the other hand, more application might produce something even better (lines 38–56). But Spencer is right to concentrate on something else instead, for there is no future in poetry; Oldham himself cannot escape, any more than the mythical ('fabulous') King Midas, who was given the terrible gift of turning all he touched to gold (lines 57–97). And yet even Aristotle (the 'Stagyrite'), to whom he turns for help, wrote an elegiac ode (lines 98–110: Oldham translated it); Oldham's compulsion could be stopped only by a Church exorcism (line 137). Then, after two sudden sexual images (the 'lecher' and the 'strange pleasure' – apparently masturbation: lines 152, 158), Oldham offers a view, intimate and amazingly articulate, of the beginnings of poetic composition (lines 162–211). The joy this brings is a delusion, though a very powerful one, and the poem ends by asking the spiritual ('ghostly') aid of his friend to 'reclaim' the Muse (line 235); the complexity of the poem has been such, however, that it is not at all clear what 'reclaiming' would mean.

Upon a Printer that Exposed-him

New Pieces. The poem appears in Oldham's autograph manuscript as 'Upon a Bookseller . . .' (publisher); the change of title reflects either a transference of the blame by Oldham, or a refusal to accept the original by Hindmarsh, his publisher. *Poems* has the manuscript title. Oldham was angry to find his *Satires upon the Jesuits* reissued in a corrupt form after he had prepared a revision; he takes a poetic revenge by threatening and cursing the guilty party.

A satirist, he declares, is not a soft target, like a love-poet, who writes to please the ladies (lines 1–8: 'Mine Hostess' is a facetious phrase, after the Chaucerian 'mine host'; Phyllis and Chloris are favourite names in love-poetry). Oldham is armed; he can act for himself, like an MP, a lawyer, or a loud-mouthed woman: in 1680, John Topham, the Serjeant-at-Arms, was directed by MPs to arrest those who breached parliamentary privilege by opposing the petitions against the Catholic Duke of York. William Scroggs (?1623–83), Lord Chief Justice, directed the jury to acquit Sir George Wakeman, a Catholic physician accused of trying to poison the King – a wildly unpopular verdict, to which Oldham refers here; the 'Coif' is the white cap worn by lawyers. Billingsgate is a London wharf famous for the verbal abuse delivered by the women selling fish (lines 27–32). Oldham's great poetic predecessors are Ovid, who wrote his poem *Ibis*, an attack on an unknown enemy, from his exile (see 'A Letter from the Country to a Friend in Town'), and Archilochus, whose lampoons drove his enemies to suicide (lines 47–51). The printer does not deserve real poetry; Oldham offers insulting alternatives: a bellman had the task of proclaiming news in a town, ringing his bell for attention. Smithfield was the home of the annual Bartholomew Fair; 'crickets' here are a kind of wooden stool, on which some low-grade entertainment is performed. 'Howard' is Edward, Dryden's brother-in-law, much mocked for his poetry. Thomas Jordan (?1612–85) wrote verse annually in honour of the Lord Mayor's Show, and was a favourite target of Oldham's. *Dutch Hudibras* (1674) was an anonymous spin-off of the original *Hudibras* by Samuel Butler (1663), which Oldham admired. The 'house' is the playhouse (lines 64–72). The printer belongs to Grub Street, a London address associated with hack-writing, such as the ghosted memoirs of criminals: Holborn was the route from Newgate prison or the Tower to the gallows at Tyburn (lines 74–6). The next destination Oldham envisages is the pillory, to which Nathaniel Reading,

Edward Christian, and Elizabeth Cellier were all condemned in 1679–80
– the first and third for reasons connected with the Popish Plot; the violent
final image of this paragraph is a brutalized borrowing from *Macbeth*, IV.
i. (30–31). From the pillory, the printer comes to prison (line 88: shoes
were one receptacle used in debtors' prisons for begging money from
passers-by). Oldham's curse ends with his victim's suicide (lines 94–5).

Imitation of Horace. Book I, Satire IX

New Pieces. This Horatian satire was imitated several times in the seventeenth century: the best-known versions are probably Act III of Ben
Jonson's play *The Poetaster* (1602), and Donne's fourth satire (published
1633). This is Oldham's first translation of a Latin satire; as with the later
ones, he creates from it a topical English poem. The Via Sacra becomes
the recently built Mall (see Waller, 'On St James's Park'), and the pest
insists on discussing the Popish Plot. The latter addition indicates a deep
divergence from the original: the Roman pest does not raise any subjects
unsettling in themselves; and Horace's praise of Maecenas and life under
his patronage has a confidence lacking from Oldham's vague mentions of
'His Grace'. The pest's parasitic ambitions, by contrast, evoke a vehemence
in Oldham lacking in the original (lines 155–6).

The poem sparkles with fashionable details. The 'Bagnio' (line 19) is
the new Turkish bath. Manly (line 24), whom the narrator longs to imitate,
is the surly hero of Wycherley's play *The Plain Dealer* (1676). The park is
St James's, which the two are crossing; the 'Groom-Porter's' was a London
gaming-house (lines 31–4). In his attempt to get away, the narrator claims
to be in 'a course' of medicine (line 41); the pest responds with an extravagant
offer (the 'Line' is the equator; the 'Cape' is the Cape of Good Hope: line
50), which switches abruptly and comically into topographical reality:
Lambeth Palace is the home of 'My Lord's' – the Archbishop of Canterbury
– just across the river from them (lines 52–3). The pest's boasting extends
over the artistic beau monde: he triumphs over Rochester, the poet (who
had died in July 1680); St André, the dancer; and Pelham Humphrey and
John Blow, leading musicians of the time (lines 68–72: after Oldham's
death, Blow would set his St Cecilia ode to music). At last they come to
Westminster Hall, where the Courts of Justice were ('Westminster' in line
87 stands for the Hall – they have been in the City of Westminster from
the start). The idea of prosecution perhaps provokes the thought of Titus
Oates, and the Jesuit seminaries at Douai and St Omers in France; Edward
Fitzharris was an Irish Catholic who tried to save himself by offering to
make revelations about Oates's plot, but was in fact hanged in July 1681,
one month after the date Oldham gives for this poem. The narrator is
noticeably cagey in his response: he has no reason for anxiety, he says, as

he does not own land which belonged to the Church before the Reformation, and thus cannot lose it if the Catholics seize power (lines 109–10). He hopes for release from the pest's crude attempts at networking when a friend appears: *Poems* explains that he is Richard Lower, Oldham's friend and a Fellow of the Royal Society, remembered for his work on blood-transfusion (pp. 421; ci–cii). But he, with a 'fleering' (leering: line 169) smile, abandons the narrator – who is saved suddenly and unexpectedly by his tormentor's arrest.

A Satire upon a Woman

Satires. The subject of this venomous piece, dated by Oldham to 1678, is not known for certain; *Poems* suggests one Lady Grey, the butt of other satires at the time (p. 406). Oldham arraigns the woman for 'Falsehood' in retracting her promise of love ('a little harmless perjury', as he imagines she might call it: line 27), and for 'unkindness' (line 12) to her former lover. These are the only charges he actually brings against her, but the flamboyant parade of curses produces an impression of monstrous vice: the poet sees himself as a partner or acting deputy for Heaven in his attack. The fierce imagery associates her with witchcraft (lines 35–7, 59–60), disease (lines 46ff., 108ff., 123ff.) and mercenary trickery (lines 23–4, 92–3: the 'squire' is a professional false witness, paid to appear at the Courts of Justice at Westminster Hall). Borrowing an insult from Donne, he compares her to a mummified corpse possessed by a devil (compare Donne, 'Love's Alchemy', line 24). Although her fault has been sexual refusal, she is accused in the language of sexual corruption (lines 64–5: the 'trade' is prostitution; lines 85–8: the 'stews' are brothels, and 'beneath', though it seems at first to mean 'under her breath', reveals on a second look a cruder, anatomical sense; lines 115ff., 142). 'Bilked' in line 142 means 'cheated'. The energy conveys an air of carnival, especially in such similes as the 'turds of quality in a gilt close-stool', that is, lavatory (line 73). But the carnival is deadly, like Bunyan's Vanity Fair: the woman is destructive because she appears attractive but is vicious at heart, just as the earth (according to one traditional theory) has Hell within it (76–7) – a parallel significantly located near the poem's own centre. His final curse is that she should not repent, but run up her soul's credit ('Tick': line 155) until it is exhausted, and die 'stupid' – in a stupor of helpless damnability (line 157).

Catullus, Epigram VII, Imitated

Poems and Translations. The epigraph is the beginning of Catullus' poem, literally translated as 'You ask how many kisses . . .'. This poem was translated and imitated often: the best-known version is the song of seduction in Ben Jonson, *Volpone*, III. vii. Line 10 is a memory of Milton's *Paradise Lost*, V. 44: 'Heaven wakes with all his eyes' – a line reported by Eve from Satan's attempt to seduce her.

A Fragment of Petronius, Paraphrased

Poems and Translations. The epigraph is literally translated: 'The pleasure in copulation is foul and short.' For the subject-matter, see Waller, 'In Answer of Sir John Suckling's Verses', and Cowley, 'Against Fruition'; Oldham's is a translation of the ancient prototype, expanded from ten lines to twenty-four with graphic language of his own.

An Ode of Anacreon Paraphrased: The Cup

Poems and Translations. For the *Anacreontea*, from which the Greek original comes, see Cowley, 'Anacreontics'. This poem is a greatly expanded version of no. 4 in the modern Loeb edition by D. A. Campbell (no. 17 in the edition known to Oldham and Cowley). Oldham was probably influenced by his pseudo-patron Rochester's version, 'Upon his Drinking a Bowl'. Oldham fills out the description with Greek legends – the battles become the Trojan War and the war brought on Thebes by the sons of Oedipus; the cup is compared to the constellation Crater, known to the Greeks. This is combined, however, with a very modern vocabulary: *Poems* notes that 'toping' (line 50) 'was still a new and fashionable word' (p. 462).

An Allusion to Martial. Book I, Epigram 118

Poems and Translations. The original is no. 117 in modern editions of Martial. The translation is close, but thoroughly modernized, so that Martial's tenement building in first-century Rome becomes a garret in Restoration Clerkenwell. This poem is the only indication we have that Oldham spent time in London; presumably he did so after leaving his school-post in Reigate in 1681.

Joseph Hindmarsh was 'Oldham's authorized publisher from the end of 1680 onward . . . His shop was at the sign of the Black Bull in Cornhill over against the Royal Exchange' (*Poems*, p. 463) (lines 15–20). He was the official publisher for the Duke of York, and published attacks on the Whig Party, enemies to the Duke. His 'posts' (line 18) are his door-posts, covered with advertisements for his books.

A Satire Addressed to a Friend

Poems and Translations. An exposé of the hardships of an impoverished intellectual, and a manifesto of independence. Oldham draws on many sources, ancient and modern. The first half draws on Juvenal, Satires V (on the degraded life of a parasite) and VII (poets are undervalued and underpaid), and Cowley's essay 'On Liberty'. For the fable in the second half, see Hammond (*John Oldham*, pp. 198–207): the sources are a Latin verse-fable by Phaedrus (first century AD) and imitations of it, including one by Oldham's French contemporary Jean de la Fontaine which may have been an inspiration for the Dog's courtliness. Out of all these, and others, Oldham creates something wholly personal and original.

The friend is poised to leave the academic life, implicitly compared to Milton's Paradise (compare line 23 with *Paradise Lost*, XII. 646). He will need more than what he has now: Aristotelian philosophy and Euclidian mathematics (traditional university subjects), or the new philosophy of René Descartes – studied in English universities from the mid century, especially in the abridged version published in 1672 by Antoine Le Grand (lines 1–10). All he has is his brain, so 'Learning' (line 35) must make his fortune; the Church is oversupplied (lines 41–3), which leaves a choice of school or private chaplaincy. The horrors of the first are summed up in the image of the 'grammar-Bridewell (line 52)': prisoners at Bridewell were beaten and set to labour – Oldham pictures schoolteaching as a life of floggings, imprisonment and grammar, with an extra (dismal) thought of marriage perhaps provoked by the prison's name (line 52). The heroes of the trade are Alexander Gill the Younger (1597–1642), a friend of Milton, High Master at St Paul's until dismissed for his addiction to beating; and Richard Busby (1605–95), Headmaster of Westminster School – generally much respected, but also a vigorous flogger (line 55). Life as a private chaplain is rather better paid, but conditions are humiliating: the address 'Sir Crape' is a sneering allusion to the thin material used for the dress of the lower clergy (line 84: bishops wore lawn, or fine linen). The chaplain must stand during dessert near the 'cistern' (apparently a bowl used for rinsing dishes at table), waiting for the 'voider' – a basket in which remains of food were collected (lines 86–9). And then another kind of grim marriage waits for him (lines 100–102). Rather than either of these, the poet fiercely embraces his poverty – 'maugre' (in spite of: line 127) his destiny. In the second half of the poem (lines 129–218), the point is reinforced by a fable. The Wolf is like 'a cast [abandoned] poet' (line 134); the Dog is like a successful candidate for the overstocked Church – a 'prebend' (line 135) is literally the stipendiary of a cathedral: a cleric of comfortable means. He eats 'costly kickshaws' – luxurious titbits – as good as the leftovers of the annual Lord Mayor's Feast (lines 149–52); he is petted like a pet lap-dog (traditionally named Shock (line 156), after their breed). The Dog is clearly a disciple of Cowley's City Mouse: both boast about their success with women (lines 163–4; compare Cowley, 'The Country Mouse', lines 40–41); both defer to their companions on the way (lines 193–4: the 'upper hand' is the place of honour; compare 'The Country Mouse', lines 60–61). But the fate of the Country Mouse is left uncertain: Oldham's Wolf escapes in time.

The Careless Good Fellow

Poems and Translations; first published on its own in 1680. Oldham writes in the person of a bluff ex-cavalier, hostile to politics, happy with the present order, loyal to his King and his pleasure; the identification of abstemiousness with sedition was made current by Royalists in the Civil War and Interregnum.

The 'plotting of late' (line 1) is a reference to the attempts by the Whig party to exclude from the throne the Duke of York, the King's Catholic brother and heir presumptive. This followed the Popish Plot scare, to which Oldham's own Jesuit satires belong, but which is here breezily dismissed as the 'rabble' in a panic (lines 3–6). To prove that his loyalty does not make him a Catholic, however, the Good Fellow mocks at the treacherous plotters, who gave up their lives for their belief. Parliament is despised – others (notably Waller) were much less easy at the recent acts for burial in woollen instead of the traditional linen (line 16). Relations with France are casually thrown in: the diplomatic duel between Henry Sidney, Whig politician, and the French ambassador, d'Avaux (line 30); and the expansionist foreign policy of Louis XIV, here a 'bully boy' or swaggerer, so different from his indolent cousin in England. The Good Fellow, that cousin's loyal subject, declines to be burnt for his beliefs at Smithfield, thus disqualifying himself as a suitable subject for the sixteenth-century Protestant martyrologist John Foxe (lines 44–5).

A Satire

Poems and Translations. Oldham draws on Juvenal, Satire VII, and other poems of complaint, adds the legend of Spenser's miserable death ('for lack of bread', according to Ben Jonson), and fills the poem with his own experiences and observations.

As the narrator sits brooding in his study, he is visited by the ghost of Spenser, looking (in Oldham's rather brutal description) like a syphilitic straight from his cure in a sweating-tub. Spenser carries his major work, *The Faerie Queene* (1590–96), but he speaks like *Mother Hubberds Tale* (1591), his short, satirical allegory of contemporary politics (lines 1–30).

He warns Oldham: any profession is better than poetry – it would be better to be a street-vendor, known to posterity only from the parish register, than Homer, poet of the *Iliad*, or Pindar, who praised the victors of chariot races in his odes (lines 31–51). There are no standards: an author sets up as a man of 'parts' (ability) even if he is only a pageant-writing hack – another dig at Thomas Jordan (see 'Upon a Printer that Exposed him') – and degrades the 'sacred name' of poet (lines 52–68). Whatever the attractions of an engraved frontispiece, showing the poet in the laurel wreath of victory (David Loggan and his pupil Robert White were the leading portrait-engravers of the time), the fame is really no more valuable than that of Titus Oates (inventor of the Popish Plot), his confederate William Bedloe, a criminal *en route* to the gallows at Tyburn (for the route via Holborn, see 'Upon a Printer that Exposed him'), or a mountebank doctor with an advertising poster (lines 69–84). Anyway, Cowley and Ben Jonson may survive, but most do not; there follows a list of forgotten poets. Of Samuel Pordage, Richard Flecknoe and Edward Howard, the first was satirized by Dryden, the second by Dryden and Marvell, the third by almost everyone (see 'Upon a Printer that Exposed him'). Francis Quarles, George Chapman, Thomas Heywood, George Wither, Robert Wild and John Ogilby were very diverse literary figures whose work included books of spiritual emblems (Quarles), translations of Homer (Chapman and Ogilby), plays (Heywood) and Puritan satires (Wither and Wild – in different styles). Joshua Sylvester is best known for his translation of Guillaume du Bartas, *Divine Weeks and Works* (1592–8), an important influence on *Paradise Lost*; James Shirley was a Caroline dramatist. Duck Lane, their new destination, was the centre of the second-hand book trade; many booksellers attended the annual Stourbridge Fair. Their poems will end as kindling for pipes ('mundungus' is inferior tobacco), as kites, or as lavatory paper (lines 85–111). The 'nice' (choosy) age will not be generous with money, even if you describe national glories, like the victories of the Black Prince or Henry V in France, which are greater than those of Virgil's hero Aeneas in Italy, or Homer's heroes at Troy; there are no modern patrons to equal Sir Philip Sidney, or the Romans Scipio and Maecenas (patrons respectively to Spenser himself, to Ennius and to Virgil, Horace and others). Even outrageous flattery gets nowhere – not even a 'tester' (small coin) is to be hoped for from a patron whose origins are in trade (one of the City Companies: line 155) but who still expects to be treated like an aristocrat (lines 112–55). This was always the case, but is now worse: Homer, said to be blind, begged for food (the 'dog and bell', traditional aids to the blind, are Oldham's addition to this old legend); the poet Sappho now would need extra income from Mother Cresswell, the famous bawd (lines 156–66). Waller had a private income; Cowley was neglected; Samuel Butler, author of the immensely popular anti-Puritan satire, *Hudibras* (1663), died in poverty (lines 167–90). Working for the theatre means dependence on the favour of the ignorant, unless one is a noble amateur, like Sir Charles Sedley. A humble professional like Elkanah Settle relies on the author's right to the proceeds of the third day's performance. Modern writers lack incentive to mug up 'rules' from Aristotle's *Poetics* or Horace's *Ars Poetica* (lines 191–226). An 'empiric', or mountebank doctor, makes a better living; the great trading companies pay well; only Parnassus, traditional home of the Muses, is a financial desert (lines 227–48). Better to become a lawyer, in the footsteps of Sir Edward Coke, Michael Dalton and Sir John Maynard (lines 249–66). But this advice is useless: a poet will not listen. Spenser ends with a curse instead: if his would-be follower persists, may he end up writing puppet-plays annually for Bartholomew Fair, and be rejected even by the Nursery Theatre – where actors were trained.

The Thirteenth Satire of Juvenal, Imitated

Poems and Translations. In the thirteenth satire, Juvenal denounces the corruption of the present age, then declares that all wrongdoing is punished in the end. This excerpt concerns impiety towards the gods: perjury; cynical abuse of the Epicurean theology (by which the gods play no part in human affairs); and belief that the gods will wait. All these ideas were topical in the Restoration; for the classic account of the ideas of an intelligent libertine, see Gilbert Burnet, *Some Passages of the Life and Death of John Earl of Rochester* (1680). The two hospitals invoked by the third liar are St Bartholomew's Hospital in West Smithfield and St Thomas's Hospital in Southwark (line 38); the 'cart' in line 55 is for conveyance to the gallows. '[O]n's' (line 64) is an abbreviation of 'on his'; 'if that' (line 65) means 'if'.

For an Anniversary of Music kept upon St Cecilia's Day

St Cecilia. Annual entertainments in honour of St Cecilia, patron saint of music, were inaugurated in 1683; Oldham's poem, published posthumously to a musical setting by John Blow, was the second. The two best-known Cecilia poems, both by Dryden, were published in 1687 and 1697. Oldham's praise of music is both sensual and spiritual, like Milton's at the end of 'L'Allegro'. For 'jubilee' (line 11), see *Satires upon the Jesuits*: Satire IV [Ignatius in Hell], line 9.

TEXTUAL VARIANTS

ABRAHAM COWLEY

On the Queen's Repairing Somerset House

line 103 This edition: kingdoms; 1668: Kingdom's

EDMUND WALLER

Of His Majesty's Receiving the News of the Duke of Buckingham's Death

line 10 1645: for Patroclus; 1664–86: of Patroclus
line 24 1645–68: the; 1682–6: their

To the Mutable Fair

line 26 Thorn Drury, *Poems,* 'in accordance with Mr Waller's manuscript': motions; 1645–86: motion

In Answer of Sir John Suckling's Verses

First heading 1645–82: Con.; 1686: Pro

On Mr John Fletcher's Plays

line 2 1647: All these good plays, but those of others too; 1645: All these good plays but those others too; 1664–86: All our good plays, and all those other too

Prologue for the Lady Actors

Maid's Tragedy Altered: Prologue for; *Second Part* Prologue to

JOHN OLDHAM

Imitation of Horace. Book I, Satire IX

line 70 1987: André; 1681: Andrew

INDEX OF TITLES

INDEX OF FIRST LINES

JOHN OLDHAM